TECHNICAL REPORT

How Much Does Military Spending Add to Hawaii's Economy?

James Hosek • Aviva Litovitz • Adam C. Resnick

Prepared for the Office of the Secretary of Defense

Approved for public release; distribution unlimited

A RAND study in cooperation with Hawaii Institute of
Public Affairs and The Chamber of Commerce of Hawaii

RAND NATIONAL DEFENSE RESEARCH INSTITUTE

The research described in this report was prepared for the Office of the Secretary of Defense (OSD). The research was conducted within the RAND National Defense Research Institute, a federally funded research and development center sponsored by OSD, the Joint Staff, the Unified Combatant Commands, the Navy, the Marine Corps, the defense agencies, and the defense Intelligence Community under Contract W74V8H-06-C-0002.

Library of Congress Control Number: 2011929136

ISBN: 978-0-8330-5267-4

The RAND Corporation is a nonprofit institution that helps improve policy and decisionmaking through research and analysis. RAND's publications do not necessarily reflect the opinions of its research clients and sponsors.

RAND® is a registered trademark.

Cover photo: Members of the U.S. Navy's flight demonstration squadron, the Blue Angels, perform aerobatic maneuvers for military and civilians during the Kaneohe Bay Air Show at Marine Corps Air Station Kaneohe Bay on Marine Corps Base Hawaii, September 25, 2010. U.S. Marine Corps photo by Lance Cpl. Tyler L. Main.

© Copyright 2011 RAND Corporation

Permission is given to duplicate this document for personal use only, as long as it is unaltered and complete. Copies may not be duplicated for commercial purposes. Unauthorized posting of RAND documents to a non-RAND website is prohibited. RAND documents are protected under copyright law. For information on reprint and linking permissions, please visit the RAND permissions page (http://www.rand.org/publications/permissions.html).

Published 2011 by the RAND Corporation
1776 Main Street, P.O. Box 2138, Santa Monica, CA 90407-2138
1200 South Hayes Street, Arlington, VA 22202-5050
4570 Fifth Avenue, Suite 600, Pittsburgh, PA 15213-2665
RAND URL: http://www.rand.org/
To order RAND documents or to obtain additional information, contact
Distribution Services: Telephone: (310) 451-7002;
Fax: (310) 451-6915; Email: order@rand.org

Preface

Defense activity in Hawaii may account for a significant portion of Hawaii's economic activity, but the relationship between defense jobs and employment in the state is not well understood. Therefore, the Hawaii Institute of Public Affairs and the Military Affairs Council of the Chamber of Commerce of Hawaii asked RAND to assess the relationship between Department of Defense (DoD) spending in Hawaii and the levels of output, employment, and earnings in Hawaii's economy.

That study, reported here, should be of interest to federal, state, and local officials, as well as to businesses and public interest organizations wishing to know about the type and level of defense spending in Hawaii and its relationship to Hawaii's economy. The approach used in this study could also be used by other states and localities to examine the role of the military in their economies.

This research was sponsored by the Office of the Secretary of Defense and conducted within the Forces and Resources Policy Center of the RAND National Defense Research Institute, a federally funded research and development center sponsored by the Office of the Secretary of Defense, the Joint Staff, the Unified Combatant Commands, the Navy, the Marine Corps, the defense agencies, and the defense Intelligence Community.

For more information on the RAND Forces and Resources Policy Center, see http://www.rand.org/nsrd/ndri/centers/frp.html or contact the director (contact information is provided on the web page).

Contents

Figures

Tables

Summary

Defense activity in Hawaii may account for a significant portion of Hawaii's economic activity, but the extent of this association has not been assessed since the publication in 1963 of a study of the relationship between defense jobs and employment in Hawaii. Therefore, the Hawaii Institute of Public Affairs and the Military Affairs Council of the Chamber of Commerce of Hawaii asked RAND to assess the relationship between DoD spending in Hawaii and the levels of output, employment, and earnings in Hawaii's economy.

RAND researchers first collected data on defense spending in Hawaii in FY 2007–2009 and then analyzed the data using the regional input-output model for Hawaii, which is maintained by the Bureau of Economic Analysis (BEA) of the U.S. Department of Commerce and was most recently updated with 2006 data. Data on defense personnel and procurement were obtained from the Defense Manpower Data Center and the Federal Procurement Data System. Personnel data comprise expenditures for active-duty personnel serving in Hawaii, members of the Hawaii Selected Reserve, and DoD civilian employees, as well as retirement benefits paid to military retirees residing in Hawaii. Defense procurement expenditure data include all contracts greater than $3,000 in which Hawaii is designated as the principal place of performance.

An input-output model describes relationships among the industries in an economy and an end-use (final) demand. The model assumes that production functions are linear, have constant returns to scale (doubling inputs doubles output), and use inputs in fixed proportions. It does not treat price adjustments in input and output markets or changes in technology. Our analysis assumes that when defense procurement and personnel dollars enter Hawaii's economy, they follow the same relationships among industries as reflected in the model. Because the model's coefficients and multipliers describe associations between final demand and output rather than causal effects, the model is useful for assessing the relationship between defense spending and Hawaii's output, earnings, and employment, but it does not consider the effect of changes in defense spending on the economy.

In this study, we treated defense spending as an end-use demand. Defense spending on procurement has a direct impact on industries in which the procurement occurs and an indirect impact on other industries. Each procurement record contains an industry code and descriptors that allowed us to map procurements to the 60 industry classes in the model. Spending on personnel acts in a similar way. DoD personnel and retirees use their wages and benefits to purchase goods and services that generate further economic activity. Data on the consumption patterns of defense personnel are not available, so we used the consumption profile in the Hawaii input-output model, adjusting it with regard to healthcare expenditures, the outflow from Hawaii of housing allowance dollars paid for privatized military housing, and per diem payments to military personnel en route to or departing from Hawaii. We used the adjusted profile to allocate defense spending on personnel to industry classes, and we adjusted the procurement profile to include DoD expenditures on the healthcare of defense personnel.

We estimated that DoD expenditures in Hawaii during FY 2007–2009 averaged $6.527 billion per year in 2009 dollars—$4.074 billion for personnel and $2.452 billion for procurement.

The expenditures were associated with $12.220 billion of output in Hawaii's economy, $3.506 billion in earnings, and full-time equivalent (FTE) employment of 101,533 people (Table S.1). The output constituted 18.4 percent of Hawaii's 2009 gross domestic product (GDP). These figures may be somewhat high, however, because of data limitations noted below.

Table S.1 also shows the average multipliers for defense spending. These are summary measures of the relationship between defense spending and output, earnings, and employment. The output multiplier for total spending (1.87) was obtained by dividing the $12.220 billion in output by the $6.527 billion total of defense spending. That is, each dollar of defense expenditure was associated with an additional 87 cents worth of output. The earnings multiplier (0.54) reflects the earnings associated with each dollar of defense expenditure. It does not include the earnings of defense personnel. The employment multiplier (16.52) indicates that 16.5 jobs were associated with each million dollars of defense expenditure. Multipliers for personnel and procurement expenditures are also given in Table S.1.

We considered the sensitivity of the estimates to a number of factors, including undercounting or overcounting defense procurement, Hawaii state taxes paid by defense personnel, the savings rate of defense personnel, Impact Aid to Hawaii schools, spending by afloat and deployed personnel, and procurement by commissaries and exchanges. The sensitivity analysis suggested that two factors, the savings rate of personnel and where the earnings of afloat and deployed personnel are spent, could decrease the results by approximately 10 percent. In addition, the consumption profile for defense personnel may not be fully accurate, as it was not specifically derived for them. Collection of original data and further analysis would be required to resolve these data limitations.

Finally, although the input-output model can provide a good assessment of the relationship between defense spending and Hawaii's output, earnings, and employment, we caution against using it as a basis for estimating the effect of a given increase or decrease in defense spending on the economy. An analysis of such a change should be based on a detailed struc-

Table S.1
Impact of Defense Expenditures on Hawaii's Economy

	Personnel	Procurement	Total
DoD expenditure (2009 $billions)	4.074	2.452	6.527
Final-demand output (2009 $billions)	7.439	4.781	12.220
Final-demand earning (2009 $billions)	1.957	1.549	3.506
Final-demand employment	61,902	39,631	101,533
Average multiplier			
Final-demand output	1.83	1.95	1.87
Final-demand earnings	0.48	0.63	0.54
Final-demand employment	16.13	17.16	16.52

NOTE: The employment multiplier is FTE employment per million dollars of expenditure in 2006 dollars (see Chapter Four).

tural model of the industries affected by the change, although this is not always practicable. Nevertheless, we caution that a $1.00 increase in defense spending will not necessarily increase Hawaii's output by $1.87.

Acknowledgments

In the course of this research, we spoke with many military and civilian officials in the Army, Navy, Marine Corps, and Air Force and at U.S. Pacific Command. We also gained valuable insights from meetings with officials at the Hawaii Institute of Public Affairs, the Chamber of Commerce of Hawaii, and the Military Affairs Council of the Chamber of Commerce of Hawaii. These meetings provided useful information about the possible impacts of defense spending, the type of data we should collect, and, more generally, the day-to-day challenges of meeting military operational requirements and taking care of service members and their families. We greatly appreciate the help of these individuals. We also would like to thank the Defense Manpower Data Center for data on active, Reserve, and DoD civilian personnel. Finally, we are grateful to our RAND reviewers, Nicholas Burger and Susan Gates, for their helpful comments.

Abbreviations

ACS	American Community Survey
BEA	U.S. Department of Commerce, Bureau of Economic Analysis
DMDC	Defense Manpower Data Center
DoD	Department of Defense
FICA	Federal Insurance Contributions Act
FTE	full-time equivalent
GDP	gross domestic product
LQ	location quotient
MTF	military treatment facility
NAICS	North American Industry Classification System
OCOLA	overseas cost of living allowance
RIMS II	Regional Input-Output Modeling System

CHAPTER ONE

Introduction

Hawaii is home to a number of major military installations[1] and more than 100,000 service members and dependents.[2] In 2009, active-duty and Department of Defense (DoD) civilian personnel comprised 10 percent of Hawaii's total employment of 661,000 (inclusive of military personnel).[3] Although defense activity may account for a significant portion of Hawaii's economic activity, the extent of the relationship between defense spending and employment in the state is not well understood.

Hawaii had a gross domestic product (GDP) of $66.4 billion in 2009 (State of Hawaii, 2011, p. 8), and military expenditures contributed to the economy both directly and indirectly, i.e., through the direct and induced demand for goods and services. This study estimates the relationship between annual average defense spending in 2007–2009 and Hawaii's output, earnings, and employment. Our estimates were made using a regional input-output model, i.e., a model that describes the relationship between the industrial sectors of the economy. In general, each industry may purchase goods and services from other industries, and each industry's output may be purchased by other industries and by end-users (consumers). The input-output model quantifies these relationships, and with data on end-user demand, the model can provide estimates of the overall output, earnings, and employment associated with that demand. In this study, we gathered suitable data for input to the model, assessed the advantages and limitations of the data and model, and produced estimates of the overall impact of defense expenditures.

We found only one prior study of the impact of the military on Hawaii (Sasaki, 1963). That study found that each additional defense job was associated with total employment of 1.28 jobs (including the defense job). Using this estimate and data from the 1950s, Sasaki projected the year-to-year change in total employment resulting from the change in defense employment in that period. Our study uses data and models that were unavailable at the time

---

[1] Fort Shafter (Headquarters of the Army Pacific Command), Schofield Barracks (home of the 25th Infantry Division), Tripler Army Medical Center, Pearl Harbor Naval Air Station, Pearl Harbor Naval Shipyard, U.S. Pacific Fleet Commander and Commander-Submarine Force, Kaneohe Marine Base, Hickam Air Force Base, Kunia Regional Security Operations Center, Camp H. M. Smith (Pacific Command Headquarters), and other, smaller installations and offices.

[2] Approximately 66,000 active-component personnel and DoD civilian employees were based in Hawaii, along with 9,000 members of the National Guard and Reserve (Defense Manpower Data Center, 2009, p. 13). There were also 55,000 active-duty dependents. The 75,000 active-duty personnel, National Guard and Reserve members, and DoD civilians, along with the active-duty dependents, constituted 10 percent of Hawaii's population of 1.3 million. In 2009, there was an overall total of 1.3 million U.S. active-duty personnel, 580,000 DoD civilians, and 830,000 National Guard and Reserve members.

[3] In 2009, Hawaii's civilian labor force numbered nearly 640,000, and its employment stood at 595,000 (State of Hawaii, 2011, Table A-1).

of Sasaki's study 50 years ago. These include detailed data on defense personnel and procurement expenditures and a regional input-output model for Hawaii.

Some data on defense expenditures are available on the Internet, but they fall short of what is required to provide accurate estimates. To illustrate, one can obtain a rough idea of the relationship between defense spending and Hawaii's economic output by assuming that Hawaii's defense spending by industry follows the same pattern as the national average (State of Hawaii, "State of Hawaii Data Book," 2009, Table 10.12).[4] But Hawaii's defense spending by industry may differ from the national average, and the relationships by industry may differ from those for the nation at large. We use detailed information on defense procurement by industry for Hawaii and specific information on expenditures on defense personnel; moreover, the input-output model is designed specifically for Hawaii.

In our approach, the defense personnel and procurement data represent end-user demands. The rationale is that, unlike industries in the input-output model, defense does not produce a good or service sold in the market; it is not an industry that sells its output to other industries or consumers. In effect, DoD is an end-user, a source of final demand. The defense expenditures fall into two broad categories, personnel and procurement. Defense personnel expenditures include compensation for active-component service members, DoD civilian employees, and members of National Guard and Reserve units, as well as benefits paid to DoD retirees living in Hawaii. These amounts, after taxes, are available to be spent on consumption. Defense procurements consist of purchases from defense contractors and also represent a final demand. In the input-output model, a given demand for a good or service leads to a direct effect, increasing the output of the industry from which the initial purchase is made, and an indirect effect because of that industry's purchases from other industries, their purchases from still other industries, and so forth. The input-output model captures these direct and indirect relationships to produce estimates of the overall relationship of defense spending to output, earnings, and employment in the economy.

Our estimates of output, earnings, and employment attributable to defense spending may be a useful reference for future studies of the role of the military in Hawaii or discussions among groups interested in the direction of Hawaii's economy. For example, the military may contribute to the development of Hawaii's research capability by bringing experts from the mainland, helping to establish research teams and initiatives with universities and research organizations, and through grants from DoD (State of Hawaii, "State of Hawaii Data Book," 2009, Table 10.06).[5] Similarly, there may be a fruitful exchange of ideas among groups concerned with access to high-quality healthcare, preschool programs, science and math teaching, and family support programs.

The structure of this study follows the data requirements of the input-output model and the nature of the available data. Figure 1.1 illustrates the study plan. Chapters Two and Three of this report present personnel and procurement data, and Chapter Four employs these data in the input-output model. Chapter Five presents our conclusions. Appendix A discusses the data sources and extraction criteria. Appendix B presents background comparisons between defense personnel and the population in Hawaii with respect to education, earnings, and family

---

[4]   Table 10.12, Impact of a $1 Billion Military Expenditure: 2010, suggests that $1 billion of defense spending will create a total output of $1.487 billion. As will be seen, our estimate differs from this number.

[5]   In 2009, DoD grants to Hawaii totaled $79 million.

Figure 1.1
Study Plan

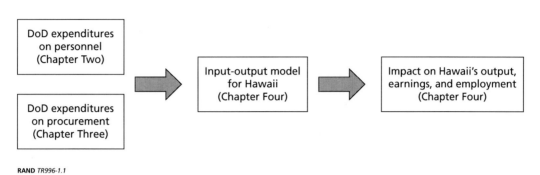

RAND *TR996-1.1*

income. Appendix C describes input-output models. Finally, Appendix D presents tables of data and input-output estimates from the analysis.

CHAPTER TWO

Defense Personnel in Hawaii and Their Earnings

Personnel expenditures make up the majority of defense spending in Hawaii and thus are a crucial component in estimating the economic impact of the military. In 2009, 75,000 individuals were serving in the military in Hawaii or were civilians employed full- or part-time by defense agencies there (Defense Manpower Data Center, 2009).[1] Earnings of these individuals, along with benefits paid to retirees, accounted for 65 percent of defense spending in the state.

This chapter begins with information on defense expenditures on personnel, or "earnings," which we adjust for taxes to arrive at earnings available for consumption. To use earnings in the input-output model, the dollar amounts must be allocated across the industry classes in the model. However, there are no data on the consumption patterns of defense personnel, so we used the consumption profile in the Hawaii input-output model. Having to assume that the consumption profile of defense personnel is the same as the Hawaii consumption profile, apart from adjustments discussed in Chapter Four, is a data limitation.

We compared education and income of defense personnel with those of the Hawaii population ages 17 and older and obtained tables from the national Consumer Expenditure Survey showing consumption profiles by age group and income group (U.S. Department of Labor, undated). These comparisons are summarized below and presented in Appendix B. The comparisons help place the defense population in the context of Hawaii's overall population.

To use these data in the model, we carry forward the after-tax personnel expenditure data from this chapter to Chapter Four, adjust the consumption profile, and use the adjusted profile to allocate personnel expenditures by industry class. Using this allocation, the model yields estimates of how this demand is related to overall output, earnings, and employment.

Defense Personnel Earnings

Table 2.1 presents pre-tax earnings of defense personnel. In FY 2007–2009, the earnings totaled $4.7 billion per year on average, in 2009 dollars. Adding retirement benefits paid out to retirees brings the total to $5.0 billion.

Active-duty earnings comprise basic pay, special and incentive pays, a cost of living allowance, and tax-exempt allowances for housing (Basic Allowance for Housing) and subsistence (Basic Allowance for Subsistence). We estimated the tax advantage and included it in the

---

[1] This estimate is based on the authors' tabulation of data from the Defense Manpower Data Center (DMDC). It differs from the 68,550 reported in the DMDC *Atlas* (DoD Personnel and Procurement Statistics, Personnel and Procurement Reports, and Data Files). Our figure is based on employment counts in the fourth quarter of 2009, and it includes Navy afloat personnel, whereas the *Atlas* figure does not.

Table 2.1
Pre-Tax Earnings of Defense Personnel ($ thousands)

Service	Active Duty	National Guard and Reserve	Civilians	Total
Army	1,441,896	119,337	334,179	1,895,413
Navy	1,046,001	7,972	676,590	1,730,562
Marine Corps	281,121	353	36,899	318,374
Air Force	387,322	61,006	142,102	590,431
Coast Guard	91,684	1,141	0	92,825
DoD			54,263	54,263
Total	3,248,024	189,810	1,244,033	4,681,867
Retiree benefits (2009)				365,265
Total annual earnings estimate				5,047,132

SOURCE: Authors' tabulations of data from Defense Manpower Data Center, 2009. Mean annual earnings for FY 2007–2009 are in FY 2009 dollars. Retirement benefits are from State of Hawaii, "State of Hawaii Data Book," 2009, Table 10.29, in 2009 dollars. Totals may not sum due to rounding.

active-duty earnings. Reservist earnings consist primarily of basic pay, although activated reservists are paid as active-duty members. We included pay to all active-duty and Reserve-component service members stationed at military installations in Hawaii regardless of their deployment status and regardless of whether or not they were afloat. DoD civilian earnings are for appropriated-fund employees only and are based on their wage or salary paid. (See Appendix A for further discussion.)

We estimated federal and state income taxes and Federal Insurance Contributions Act (FICA) deductions and subtracted them from gross earnings to obtain after-tax earnings (see Table 2.2). After-tax annual earnings are estimated to be $4.2 billion. Not all earnings are consumed—some may be saved, but we do not have data on the savings rate of defense personnel. We discuss this limitation further in Chapter Four.

Table 2.2
Tax Estimates and Net Earnings of Defense Personnel ($ thousands)

Gross earnings	5,047,132
Less	
Federal taxes	450,451
State taxes	113,046
FICA	290,166
Net earnings	4,193,468

SOURCE: Authors' tabulations of data from Defense Manpower Data Center, 2009. American Community Survey (ACS) data for 2007–2009 (Ruggles et al., 2010) were also used to estimate mean annual amounts for FY 2007–2009 in FY 2009 dollars. Totals may not sum due to rounding.

How Many Defense Personnel Are in Hawaii?

Table 2.3 presents numbers of defense personnel obtained from privacy-protected personnel files from DMDC. More than 75,000 people served in the military or were employed by DoD in Hawaii in 2009. There were 48,000 active-duty service members, 18,000 DoD civilian employees, and 9,000 National Guard and Reserve members. Sixty-three percent of defense personnel are active-duty service members, and of these, 15 percent are officers and 85 percent are enlisted. The National Guard and Reserve members constitute 12 percent of defense personnel, and DoD civilians constitute 24 percent. (Totals do not sum to 100 percent because of rounding.) DoD civilian employees shown in Table 2.3 are appropriated-fund employees; non–appropriated-fund employees are not included.

Figure 2.1 shows the trend in the number of defense personnel in Hawaii. The number peaked in 1985. The United States began a force size reduction in the late 1980s and continued it after the Cold War ended. By 1996, U.S. active and Reserve strength had decreased by one-third. In Hawaii, the number of defense personnel fell from 68,000 in 1990 to 56,000 in 1999 and stayed at that level for eight years. By 2008, the total had grown to 60,000. That figure does not include personnel afloat[2] or reservists, so the number of personnel in Figure 2.1 (60,000) is less than the 75,000 in Table 2.3. Still, the trends in the figure are probably accurate. Also, given the 15,000-person difference and the Table 2.3 estimate of 9,400 reservists, there may have been 5,600 afloat personnel.[3]

How Many Military Retirees Are in Hawaii?

There were 16,088 military retirees residing in Hawaii in 2009 (State of Hawaii, "State of Hawaii Data Book," 2009). The retirees are part of Hawaii's total veteran population of 117,000 (Ruggles et al., 2010). In 2009, veterans constituted 9 percent of the population of Hawaii ages 16 and older. (DoD civilian employee retirees are not considered military retirees. Their

Table 2.3
Defense Personnel in Hawaii, FY 2009

Service	Active Duty	National Guard and Reserve	DoD Civilian	Total
Army	21,421	5,380	5,529	32,330
Navy	14,237	821	8,902	23,960
Marine Corps	6,026	77	687	6,790
Air Force	4,621	3,028	2,190	9,839
Coast Guard	1,372	121		1,493
Other DoD			1,061	1,061
Total	47,677	9,427	18,369	75,473

SOURCE: Authors' tabulations of data from DMDC for FY 2009.

---

[2]   Afloat personnel include sailors and Marines on board a ship but based in Hawaii.

[3]   Time series data on Hawaii Army National Guard and Air National Guard, the two biggest Hawaii Reserve components, indicate about 5,800 reservists in the mid-1980s, 5,400 circa 2000, and 4,970 in 2007 (State of Hawaii, "State of Hawaii Data Book," 2009, Table 10.14). These counts are lower than the counts in Table 2.3, although both are based on DoD data. A reservist count of, say, 6,000 in 2009 would imply 9,000 afloat personnel. In contrast, the count in the table suggests an estimate of 5,600 (15,000 − 9,400).

Figure 2.1
Defense Personnel in Hawaii, 1982–2009

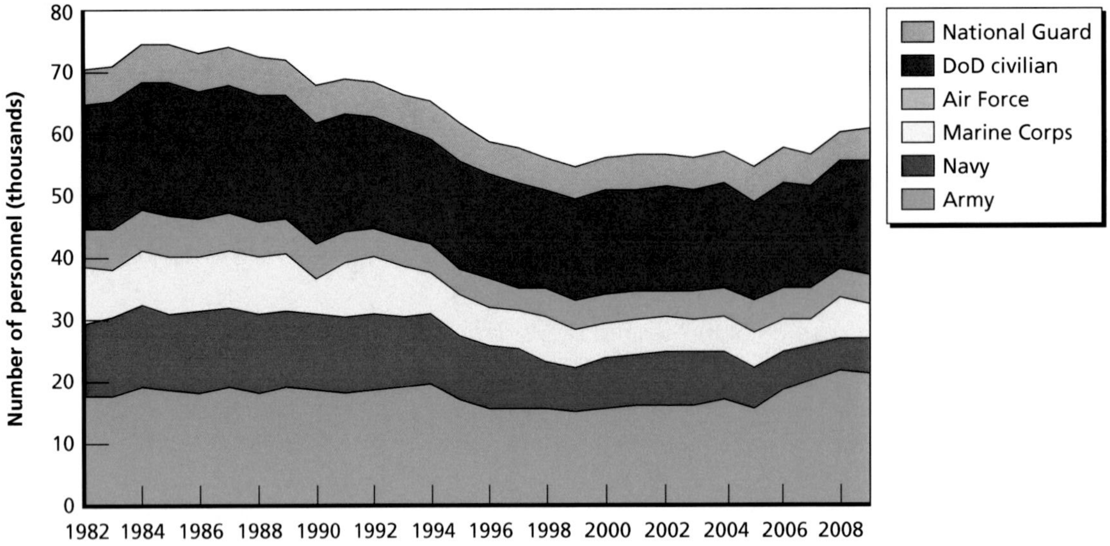

SOURCE: State of Hawaii, "State of Hawaii Data Book," 2009, Tables 10.03, 10.11, 10.14.
RAND *TR996-2.1*

retirement benefits are paid not by DoD but through the Federal Employees Retirement System.)

How Do Defense Personnel Compare with the Population of Hawaii?

We compared personnel data from DMDC with ACS data on Hawaii's population with respect to age, gender, education, individual earnings, and family income. These comparisons are presented in Appendix B and summarized here.

The Hawaii active-duty population is younger than the Hawaii adult population: 92 percent of active-duty service members are under 40 years of age. Most active-duty members are male (86 percent), and most are enlisted (85 percent).

In 2009, 86 percent of enlisted personnel had a high school education, 12 percent had more than a high school education, and 2 percent had less than a high school education. Among officers, 54 percent had four years of college, 42 percent had post-graduate education, and 4 percent had less than four years of college. Grouping officers and enlisted personnel together, 73 percent had finished high school, 7 percent had some college education, 12 percent had four years of college, 7 percent had post-graduate education, and 1 percent had less than a high school education. Among DoD civilians, 38 percent had a high school education, 25 percent had some college education, 35 percent had a four-year college degree or higher, and 2 percent had less than a high-school education. The educational attainment of National Guard and Reserve members is similar to that of DoD civilians, but with slightly lower college levels. In the Hawaii population ages 17 and older, 38 percent had a high school education, 25 percent had some college education, 26 percent had four or more years of college, and 11 percent did not have a high school diploma.

Active-duty service members and DoD civilian employees earned more on average than Hawaii's full-time workforce. In 2007–2009, median earnings for active-duty personnel were $74,900, and those for DoD civilians were $69,800 (2009 dollars). The median earnings of full-time workers in Hawaii were $40,000 (ages 17 and older) or $37,400 (ages 17 to 50).[4] Members of the National Guard and Reserve earned $20,135 as reservists (inactive and activated).

Incomes of families of defense personnel are similar to those of Hawaii families with a full-time worker. Families with a full-time worker often have multiple workers plus family income other than wages. Active-duty family income is only slightly higher than service member individual earnings, because of lower labor force participation, employment, and wages of active-duty spouses (Hosek et al., 2002). Median family income was $87,300 for active-duty personnel, $85,000 for Hawaii families with a full-time worker ages 17 and older, and $80,500 for Hawaii families with a full-time worker ages 17 to 50.

How Does Consumption Vary by Age and Income?

The comparisons above establish that defense personnel are younger, have modal education of high school, and have incomes similar to those of Hawaii families with a full-time worker. Table 2.4 presents consumption data for three age groups, and Table 2.5 presents consumption data for five income groups. The data are from the Consumer Expenditure Survey (U.S. Department of Labor, undated), which is, however, a survey of the overall population, not a military-specific population. The tables show that consumption shares (percentages) change "moderately" across age and income; many changes are less than a percentage point, although some are several percentage points. Food, housing, transportation, and personal insurance and pensions account for 75 percent or more of consumption expenditures.

The shares by category change somewhat across age groups. For example, the share of spending on food is 13.5 percent at 25–34 years and at 35–44 years, and 12.7 percent at 45–54

Table 2.4
Share of Spending for Consumption Categories by Age Groups (percentage)

Item	25–34 Years	35–44 Years	45–54 Years
Food	13.5	13.5	12.7
Alcohol	1.0	0.9	0.9
Housing and housekeeping	37.1	36.1	32.4
Apparel and services	4.0	4.1	3.2
Transportation	16.5	14.6	16.0
Healthcare	3.9	4.4	5.4
Entertainment	5.4	5.8	5.4
Personal care	1.2	1.2	1.1
Education	1.7	1.6	3.5
Smoking products and supplies	0.8	0.7	0.9
Miscellaneous	1.4	1.7	1.8
Cash contributions	2.2	2.8	3.5
Personal insurance and pensions	11.4	12.4	13.0

SOURCE: U.S. Department of Labor, undated.

---

[4]   The Hawaii figures exclude individuals on active duty. However, reservists are not excluded. Hawaii workers who are also reservists are a small percentage of Hawaii's labor force, approximately 1.5 percent (9,400/640,000).

Table 2.5
Share of Spending for Consumption Categories by Income Groups (percentage)

Item	Annual Income (2009 dollars)				
	70,000–79,999	80,000–99,999	100,000–119,999	120,000–149,000	150,000 or more
Food	13.5	12.9	12.6	11.5	10.6
Alcohol	0.9	0.9	1.0	1.0	1.0
Housing and housekeeping	33.1	33.3	31.4	32.5	31.2
Apparel and services	3.1	3.7	3.4	3.4	3.6
Transportation	17.1	15.3	16.3	15.2	14.3
Healthcare	6.4	6.4	5.8	5.1	4.2
Entertainment	5.8	5.6	6.1	5.6	5.8
Personal care	1.1	1.2	1.3	1.3	1.2
Education	1.4	1.9	2.4	2.8	3.9
Smoking products and supplies	0.8	0.6	0.5	0.4	0.3
Miscellaneous	1.7	1.5	1.7	1.6	1.7
Cash contributions	2.9	3.7	3.2	3.5	4.8
Personal insurance and pensions	12.0	12.9	14.1	15.8	17.1

SOURCE: U.S. Department of Labor, undated.

years, 36.1 percent at 35–44 years, and 32.4 percent at 45–54 years. In the 45–54-year group, relatively more is spent on healthcare, education, cash contributions, and personal insurance and pensions. But the shares change little between the 25–34 and 35–44-year groups.

Most DoD civilians and active-duty personnel are in the lower two income groups shown, $70,000–$79,999 and $80,000–$99,999. The food share of spending declines from 13.5 percent at $70,000–$79,999, 12.9 percent at $80,000–$99,999, 12.6 percent at $100,000–119,999, and 11.5 percent at $120,000–$149,000. For incomes of $150,000 or more, the food share is 10.6 percent. The transportation share decreases with income, while the shares for education, cash contributions, and personal insurance and pensions increase.

Summary

Defense personnel expenditures in Hawaii, measured by after-tax earnings of 75,000 defense personnel and including benefits paid to military retirees, averaged $4.2 billion per year in 2007–2009. These estimates are used in Chapter Four to find Hawaii's output, earnings, and employment associated with the expenditures.

CHAPTER THREE

Defense Procurement in Hawaii

We obtained data on defense procurement for FY 2007–2009 from the Federal Procurement Data System for contracts in which Hawaii is the principal place of performance.[1] This chapter presents these data by contracting agency, over time, by Hawaii county, by vendor address (Hawaii, non-Hawaii), and for the 15 largest industry classes.[2]

Defense Procurement Expenditures

Defense procurements averaged $2.3 billion per year in FY 2007–2009 in 2009 dollars (Table 3.1). Purchases by the Navy and Army accounted for 73 percent of the total, or nearly $1.7 billion.

Defense procurements in Hawaii were relatively constant from 1982 to 1995, then they grew steadily to the present (Figure 3.1). Procurements totaled $910 million in 1995, $1.4 billion in 2000, $2.2 billion in 2005, and almost $2.4 billion in 2009. Average annual procurement (obtained from the prime-contract trend data) was $2.307 billion for 2007–2009.[3]

Table 3.1
Annual Average Procurement by DoD Agency, FY 2007–2009

Contracting Agency	Average Annual Procurement (2009 dollars)
Department of the Navy	954,043,106
Department of the Army	734,050,645
Department of the Air Force	292,510,262
Defense Logistics Agency	207,063,944
Defense Information Systems Agency	55,893,418
Defense Commissary Agency	45,563,458
U.S. Coast Guard	17,702,402
All agencies	2,306,827,235

SOURCE: Authors' tabulations of data from Federal Procurement Data System, undated.

---

[1] Federal Procurement Data System, undated. See Appendix A.

[2] Not all Hawaii procurement dollars stay in Hawaii's economy. The input-output model allows for the fact that goods and services may be supplied locally or may come from the mainland.

[3] The data in Figure 3.1 are for prime contracts; until FY 2001, the minimum contract was $25,000, though that was relaxed in later years.

Figure 3.1
DoD Prime Contracts in Hawaii, 1982–2009

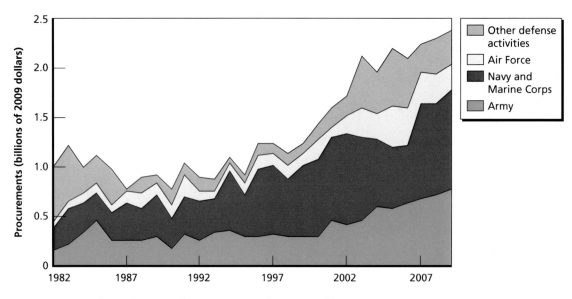

SOURCES: State of Hawaii, "State of Hawaii Data Book," 2011, Table 10.18; U.S. Department of Commerce, undated.

Hawaii-based procurement varied across counties, ranging from $10 million and $27 million in Maui and Hawaii counties, respectively, to $106 million in Kauai and $2.162 billion in Honolulu (Table 3.2). Honolulu County accounted for 94 percent of total procurement.

Defense procurements for which Hawaii is the principal place of performance are made from both Hawaii and non-Hawaii vendors. We use both in our analysis. A Hawaii vendor is defined as a vendor whose address on the vendor contract is in the state of Hawaii.

Overall, 58 percent of procurement expenditures went to vendors with an address in Hawaii (Table 3.3). Defense Commissary Agency procurement totaled $45 million, 92 percent of which went to Hawaii vendors, by far the highest percentage. In contrast, Air Force procurement was nearly $300 million, of which 30 percent went to Hawaii vendors. This percentage is comparatively low, in part, because 54 percent of Air Force procurement was in the category of professional, scientific, and technical services, for which 76 percent of overall procurement was from non-Hawaii vendors. Procurements from Hawaii vendors totaled 62 percent for the Navy and 57 percent for the Army.

Table 3.2
Annual Average Procurement by County, FY 2007–2009

County	Average Annual Procurement (2009 dollars)
Honolulu	2,162,447,438
Kauai	106,018,965
Hawaii	27,058,459
Maui	10,104,249
Unidentified	3,592,050
All counties	2,309,221,161

SOURCE: Authors' tabulations of data from the Federal Procurement Data System, undated.

Table 3.3
Average Annual Procurement by DoD Agency and Vendor Address, FY 2007–2009

Contracting Agency	Annual Procurement (2009 dollars)		Percentage of Procurement from Vendors with Hawaii Address
	Vendors with Hawaii Address	Vendors with Address Outside Hawaii	
Defense Commissary Agency	41,728,066	3,835,380	92
Defense Logistics Agency	148,825,845	58,238,048	72
Defense Information Systems Agency	35,826,362	20,067,041	64
Department of the Navy	593,357,836	360,375,143	62
Department of the Army	421,634,765	312,415,649	57
U.S. Coast Guard	10,159,286	7,543,107	57
Department of the Air Force	88,180,103	204,330,051	30
All Agencies	1,339,712,262	966,804,419	58

SOURCE: Authors' tabulations of data from Federal Procurement Data System, undated.

Procurement by Category

Each procurement record contains a North American Industry Classification System (NAICS) code, which we used to assign the procurements into the 60 different industry classes of the input-output model. These classes vary in their economic impact, so an accurate allocation is valuable for our estimation. Twelve classes accounted for 92 percent of annual average procurement in FY 2007–2009, and 15 classes accounted for 95 percent. Table 3.4 lists the industry

Table 3.4
Average Annual Procurement for the 15 Largest Industry Classes, FY 2007–2009

Industry Class	Average Annual Procurement (2009 dollars)	Cumulative Percentage
7. Construction	787,163,568	35
47. Professional, scientific, and technical services	456,915,563	56
49. Administrative and support services	192,104,808	64
24. Petroleum and coal products manufacturing	176,656,356	72
16. Other transportation equipment manufacturing	90,191,358	76
6. Utilities	79,539,542	80
50. Waste management and remediation services	66,631,536	83
27. Wholesale trade	61,247,417	85
52. Ambulatory healthcare services	57,697,537	88
59. Other services	34,223,933	90
28. Retail trade	30,549,285	91
35. Other transportation and support activities	24,872,857	92
19. Food, beverage, and tobacco product manufacturing	24,192,320	93
13. Computer and electronic product manufacturing	22,879,929	94
51. Educational services	17,954,935	95
Total	2,122,820,945	
Total procurement (all classes)	2,237,207,270	

SOURCE: Authors' tabulations of data from the Federal Procurement Data System, undated.

classes by number and name, the amount of procurement, and the cumulative percentage of procurement. The largest classes were construction; professional, scientific, and technical services; and administrative and support services. These classes accounted for 64 percent of procurement in 2007–2009, and construction alone accounted for 35 percent. Petroleum and coal products manufacturing accounted for 8 percent, and the remaining classes, which accounted for 2 percent to 4 percent each, included other transportation equipment manufacturing, utilities, waste management and remediation services, wholesale trade, ambulatory healthcare services, telecommunications, other services, and retail trade.

Summary

DoD procurement in which Hawaii was the principal place of performance averaged $2.3 billion annually in FY 2007–2009. Honolulu County accounted for 94 percent of total procurement, and vendors with addresses in Hawaii accounted for 58 percent. Four of the 60 industry classes accounted for 72 percent of total procurement, and 10 classes accounted for 90 percent.

CHAPTER FOUR

Economic Modeling

To examine the impact of defense spending on Hawaii's economy, we used the regional input-output model for Hawaii from the U.S. Department of Commerce, Bureau of Economic Analysis (BEA) Regional Input-Output Modeling System (RIMS II), which is based on 2006 data. In this chapter we describe economic analysis with an input-output model and the way BEA adapts the model for regional economic analysis. We discuss adjustments to the defense expenditure data, the estimates from the input-output model, and the sensitivity of those estimates to further possible adjustments.

Input-Output Models

Input-output models are linear equations describing an industry's output in terms of its demand for (purchases of) the outputs of other industries and its own value added, plus the end-user demand for its output. Input-output models quantify the input-output relationships among all industries and include end-user demand; the model for Hawaii shows the relationship between defense spending and Hawaii's output, earnings, and employment. Input-output models have been used for a variety of analyses such as estimating the effect of adding a sports stadium to a local economy or changing the mix of industries, though we caution that more-specific "structural" models may be better for such purposes. The fact that input-output models include end-user demand is valuable for our study because procurement is an end-user demand by DoD, and expenditures on defense personnel translate into end-user consumer demand.[1]

Construction of an input-output model begins with setting up a matrix representing the technology used to produce goods and services in the national economy. The matrix consists of a set of industries arrayed in rows as the producing sectors, and the same set of industries arrayed in columns as the consuming industries. An industry produces its output with inputs from itself and inputs purchased from some or all of the other industries (rows). An industry also supplies its output to other industries, and the column for an industry reflects how its output is consumed by other industries and by itself. The rows and columns for the industries are called the producer portion of the national input-output model. This matrix is augmented with a household column and a household row to account for consumer demand. In addition, the model includes a column of total output by industry and a column of final demand

---

[1] The amount spent on consumption will equal expenditures on defense personnel net of taxes and savings. In Table 2.2, estimated taxes are deducted from gross earnings. Savings should also be deducted, but data on defense personnel savings are not available. We assume zero savings in our initial analysis and consider positive savings in the subsection on sensitivity analyses.

by industry. The model can be extended to include other columns, e.g., the RIMS II includes columns to project the earnings and employment associated with overall output. The model is solved to compute the overall impact on output, earnings, and employment deriving from end-user demand—in this study, from defense spending.

BEA creates regional input-output models from the national input-output model by using data on the structure of the regional economy based on information on regional earnings or personal income. (Appendix B describes BEA's approach.) The regional earnings and income data are used to infer the regional industry's capacity to meet regional demand.

Input-output models are based on simplifying assumptions. One assumption is that production technology is additively separable without interactions between the inputs to an industry. This assumption is strong (restrictive), because it does not permit substitution of one input for another in response to changes in their prices and because it assumes that a doubling of inputs doubles output. These assumptions make the input-output model most suitable for projections under conditions where input price changes and technology are constant or nearly so. A large, rapid change in aggregate demand or demand for an industry's output could cause input prices and technology to change, but the model does not address such adjustments. The RIMS II model, like other input-output models, is a "static equilibrium model" (U.S. Department of Commerce, 1997, p. 8).[2] The model can be thought of as providing a first-order approximation to a more complex underlying technology; a first-order approximation is likely to be more accurate, the smaller the change in the relevant variable, e.g., final demand.

The model uses information on the sales and purchases of businesses and aggregates this information by industry. Although the model offers a cohesive framework for viewing these flows and their relationship to final demand, this is not the same as identifying the underlying structural relationships or showing the causal effect of a given change in demand or production. The model is not designed to estimate the effect of changes in defense spending on the economy.

Nevertheless, the RIMS II model is appropriate for assessing the relationship between defense spending and Hawaii's output, earnings, and employment given current prices, wages, and technology. Military spending in Hawaii has increased in the past decade, but the increase has been gradual. Further, Hawaii's economy has likely been evolving and growing gradually, as have other states' economies. For instance, although unemployment in Hawaii decreased, then increased in the past decade, the swings have been less than those of the national economy, which suggests less pressure for wage adjustment. Hawaii's unemployment rate was between 5 and 6 percent from 1994 to 1999; it declined in the early part of the following decade, reaching 2 to 3 percent in 2006–2008, then increased to 6 to 7 percent between 2008 and 2009 as the recession took hold. Finally, it decreased to 5.8 percent in December 2010, when the national rate of unemployment was 9.1 percent. Hawaii is a small part of the national and global markets that determine prices, so it has little effect on prices. Producer prices have been fairly stable through the decade, although there has been volatility in certain areas such as energy, gold, and food. To be consistent with the linear cost effects in the RIMS II model, we must assume

---

[2] In general, a large increase in demand for a product might drive up the cost of the product. The increase in cost could come from higher input prices (i.e., an increasing marginal cost of inputs), decreasing returns to scale in production (holding input prices constant, doubling input would less than double output), or managerial or capital constraints. For example, an electricity producer may have a constrained capacity to produce electricity from its most efficient plants. If consumers demand a greater amount of electricity, the producer must turn to less-efficient plants. When the manufacturer increases its total production quantity and utilizes its more-expensive plants, the average cost per unit of electricity will increase.

that the direct effect of defense spending on Hawaii's economy is small enough to cause little change in input prices and hence the marginal cost at which goods and services are produced in Hawaii. As shown in Figures 2.1 and 3.1, procurement and personnel expenditures have been stable for the past few years.

However, the level of resolution of the input-output model is the industry class, and the regional model has 60 industry classes, whereas the industry classification system has five-digit categories. This suggests that an input-output model is likely to give a more accurate estimate for a demand change that broadly affects the companies within an industry than for a change that affects particular companies, since their output, earnings, and employment response might differ from the industry average. By implication, having more specific information about industry technology, prices, and capacity would enable a more precise estimate of the effects of changes in demand or investment targeted on narrowly defined portions of an industry.

Personnel expenditures enter Hawaii's economy as consumer purchases that presumably affect many industries broadly. Procurement expenditures in 2007–2009, however, were concentrated. Fifteen industries accounted for 95 percent of procurement, and three industries alone (construction; professional, scientific, and technical services; and administrative and support services) accounted for 64 percent. It is likely that procurement affects these industries broadly, whereas industries with 2 to 3 percent of procurement but still in the top 15 might be more narrowly affected. The remaining 45 industries in the model account for 5 percent of procurement. Procurements are unlikely to have a broad effect on these industries, and model estimates are likely to be less accurate. Still, we do not know in detail how all industries actually do business with DoD. For instance, 35 percent of procurement went to the construction industry, and if a construction company with a DoD contract purchased more of its inputs from the mainland than a typical construction company did, the input-output model will overestimate the impact on Hawaii's output, earnings, and employment. This limitation cannot be overcome without original data collection and further analysis.

The other main assumption in input-output models is that goods and services produced by industries cannot be substituted in production or consumption. Zero substitution is implied by the structure of the model in that it assumes each industry uses a fixed combination of outputs from selected industries to produce its output. We expect that DoD activity in Hawaii will not cause Hawaii's industries to dramatically change their production technology or prices in the near term, which is consistent with the assumption of zero substitution between outputs.

Our Inputs to the Model

Our raw inputs to the RIMS II model for Hawaii were described in Chapters Two and Three. Using data from DMDC, we estimated that after-tax earnings of defense personnel and benefits paid to military retirees totaled $4.2 billion per year, on average, for 2007–2009. Using data from the Federal Procurement Data System, we estimated that defense procurements in which Hawaii was the principal place of performance were $2.3 billion per year, on average, during this period.

The earnings and procurement data must be refined before they can be used in the input-output model. The steps in the refinement process include the following:

- Make an initial allocation to industry classes. For procurement data, we mapped each vendor record into one of the 60 industry classes in RIMS II based on the six-digit industry classification code and descriptive fields on the record (see Appendix A). For earnings data, we allocated the total amount of after-tax earnings to the industry classes according to the consumption shares in RIMS II. These shares are based on economic activity viewed from the industry perspective and differ from the consumer-expenditure shares based on the U.S. Department of Labor's Consumer Expenditure Survey.
- Refine the allocation to adjust for transportation cost, wholesale margin, and retail margin. For example, for every dollar spent on food, beverage, and tobacco product manufacturing, 57 cents go to the manufacturer, 1 cent goes to transportation (mainly trucking), 12 cents go to wholesalers, and 29 cents go to retailers (according to RIMS II). Thus, 1 cent is moved from the food, beverage, and tobacco class to the truck transportation class, 12 cents to wholesale trade, and 29 cents to retail trade. RIMS II supplies the factors for these adjustments.
- Make further refinements, discussed below.

The final step is multiplying the refined allocations by industry class by the RIMS II final-demand multipliers for output, earnings, and employment to obtain the impact on the economy. The multipliers are created by solving the model (see Appendix C); they indicate the overall impact on output, earnings, and employment per dollar of end-user demand.

The RIMS II model uses year 2006 dollars. To estimate employment impacts in the model, we converted our data to 2006 dollars, as the use of 2009 dollars would have given an inflated estimate of employment. For output, earnings, and the average multipliers we computed, the use of 2009 dollars is fully accurate.

Adjustments

The consumption profile in the model may not be accurate for defense personnel. We adjusted it in several ways, i.e., for privatized military housing costs, travel-related expenses as active-duty personnel move to and from Hawaii, and healthcare expenses. We also considered adjusting it for commissaries and exchanges and transportation expenses of mainland visitors but did not do so.

Many active-duty service members live on base, and their spending on housing could have a different effect on the local economy than that of members living off base. Active-component service members receive a housing allowance regardless of whether they live off or on base. If they live off base, they can spend the housing allowance as they wish, not necessarily on housing. Service members living off base typically rent their housing. Those who live on base "rent" from the government, and their housing allowance is automatically deducted from their earnings. In the Air Force, almost 50 percent of active-duty service members live on base (Hickam Air Force Base, 2008).

Much of the military housing in Hawaii has been recently constructed, and most of it is privatized.[3] Since 2004, the private sector has constructed, renovated, and managed 16,925

---

[3] All housing at Hickam has been privatized. All Navy and Marine Corps housing in Hawaii operates under a public-private venture. Most, if not all, of Army housing is privatized (Office of the Deputy Assistant Secretary of Defense for Military Community and Family Policy, 2011).

units. Forest City provides Navy and Marine Corps units, and Actus Lend Lease provides Army and Air Force units (Office of the Deputy Under Secretary of Defense, undated). These companies design, build, manage, and maintain military housing and earn a return on their military housing investment through housing allowance payments. The military housing payments enter the private sector as rent for off-base apartments would. However, Forest City and Actus are national companies, and a relatively high portion of the housing payments they receive may be sent to the mainland. This might also be true of off-base rentals from large companies but not of rentals from small companies or "mom and pop"-owned rental units. We assume that roughly half of the active-duty members live on base (24,000) and receive an average housing allowance of $2,024 per month,[4] for a total of $583 million per year (2009 dollars). Allowing for ongoing operations and maintenance, we assume that one-fourth of this amount, which is not taxable, leaves Hawaii. To adjust for this, we subtract $146 million from the amount initially allocated to real estate in the consumption profile of DoD personnel. This is a conservative adjustment in the sense that it is in addition to the amount the model already assumes leaves Hawaii.

Service members relocating to or from Hawaii may spend a few days vacationing alone or with their families. Like tourism, this may involve hotels, taxis, and dining out. Military families move about three times more often than comparable civilian families (Hosek et al., 2002), so they may spend a higher share of their income on travel or tourism-related activities. Service members on the move receive a per diem, the maximum amount of which in 2009 was $283 in the Honolulu area, $219 at Hilo and Kilauea military camp, and $313 at Kauai and Kekaha missile range facility (Defense Travel Management Office, "Per Diem Rates Query," undated). We added $27 million to the initial allocation of consumption, splitting it among food services and accommodation.[5]

Spending at exchanges and military commissaries adds to Hawaii's employment. However, not all spending at commissaries results from military spending on personnel and procurement, and our focus is on the latter. If service members and military retirees make a high percentage of their consumer purchases at commissaries and exchanges, employment at these outlets will increase, but employment at other retail outlets will decrease. Also, some of this spending may come from earnings or income from sources other than DoD; for example, retirees' spending at commissaries and exchanges will depend on their total income, not just their retirement benefits.

Further, we are interested in the relationship between defense spending and Hawaii's overall output, employment, and earnings, and the input-output model captures this overall impact. Some employment reflects workers hired by commissaries and exchanges, and some reflects workers hired elsewhere in the economy. The model does not identify effects at this level. Nevertheless, we think the model captures the overall impacts of defense spending.

---

[4]   We based this on 2009 Hawaii Basic Allowance for Housing rates for an E5 (sergeant) and an O4 (major); we assumed that half had dependents and half did not, and that 85 percent were enlisted. Basic Allowance for Housing rates are from Defense Travel Management Office, "BAH Calculator," undated.

[5]   If one-third of active-duty personnel move each year, 16,000 service members would arrive in Hawaii, and the same number would depart. If each received three days of per diem in Hawaii, this would add $27,168,000 [(16,000 + 16,000) × 3 × 283]. In addition, service members may receive a temporary lodging allowance while they are seeking housing or awaiting on-post housing. We have not included that allowance. DoD deducts (nets out) 1/30 of the monthly housing allowance for each day of temporary lodging allowance.

As a related point, some of the employment impact may reflect Hawaii businesses hiring military spouses. As members of Hawaii's labor force, military spouses are included in the model's estimates. We make a rough estimate of this below.

Active-duty service members, activated reservists, their families, and military retirees are eligible for healthcare through the military healthcare system, TRICARE. Healthcare is received by service members at no cost and by dependents and retirees at low cost. Active-duty members receive their care on base at military treatment facilities (MTFs), while dependents and retirees may receive care at MTFs or through civilian providers. The costs of this healthcare are not included in the earnings or procurement data, but they should be. We contacted TRICARE and learned that in FY 2009, the cost of purchased care was $72 million. This is the amount TRICARE paid healthcare providers for care provided outside of the MTFs. To adjust for the military healthcare system, in our initial allocation of earnings to consumption, we assume that active-duty members and military retirees have zero out-of-pocket costs for healthcare and spend their earnings in other categories. We also add $72 million to procurement expenditures allocated to healthcare.

DoD civilians receive healthcare through the Federal Employees Health Benefit Program. We assume they spend 5 percent of their after-tax earnings on healthcare. This percentage is in line with the percentages in the Consumer Expenditure Survey. We estimate $52 million in out-of-pocket expense[6] and use this amount in constructing the initial allocation of consumption expenditures. DoD, as the employer, pays most of the cost of healthcare. We estimate DoD's contribution to be $143 million per year,[7] and we add this amount to procurement expenditures allocated to healthcare.

We also assume that members of the National Guard and Reserve spend 5 percent of their DoD earnings on healthcare, and their private sector employer pays the remainder of their healthcare costs; this amount does not enter into our analysis.

DoD agencies purchase many items on the mainland and ship them to Hawaii. These purchases are not included in the procurement data, but their shipment presumably brings more ships and crews to Hawaii and has some effect on its economy. We made no adjustment for this.

Results

Using the RIMS II multipliers, we calculated the effect of annual defense expenditures for 2007–2009 on Hawaii's economy. Results are shown in Table 4.1. The first row of the table presents defense expenditures, including the adjustments discussed for personnel, procurement, and the total. The next three rows show the model estimates of the effects of these

---

[6] Table 2.1 shows pre-tax earnings of DoD civilians of $1.244 billion. Using the tax adjustment in Table 2.2, we estimate after-tax earnings of $1.042 billion; 5 percent of this is $52 million.

[7] The government cost in 2009 for healthcare at Kaiser Permanente Hawaii was $302.57 per month for single coverage and $650.55 for family coverage. The other health maintenance organization in Hawaii (Blue Cross/Blue Shield) is slightly cheaper. The government cost for Blue Cross/Blue Shield in 2009 was $281.75 for single coverage and $627.14 for family coverage in the standard option (not limited to the preferred provider network) and $277.32/$649.45 in the basic option. We assumed DoD civilian employees had family coverage at a government cost of $650 per month. The annual cost for the 18,369 civilian employees was thus $143,278,200. The government costs for the Federal Employees Health Benefit Program came from U.S. Office of Personnel Management, undated.

Table 4.1
Impact of Defense Expenditures on Hawaii's Economy

	Personnel	Procurement	Total
DoD expenditure (2009 $billions)	4.074	2.452	6.527
Final-demand output (2009 $billions)	7.439	4.781	12.220
Final-demand earnings (2009 $billions)	1.957	1.549	3.506
Final-demand employment	61,902	39,631	101,533
Average multiplier			
Final-demand output	1.83	1.95	1.87
Final-demand earnings	0.48	0.63	0.54
Final-demand employment	16.13	17.16	16.52

expenditures for the economy, taking account of direct and indirect relationships. Total defense expenditures of $6.527 billion were associated with $12.220 billion of economic output, $3.506 billion of earnings, and 101,533 jobs.[8] About one-third of these amounts came from procurement and two-thirds from earnings. To place the output in context, Hawaii's annual GDP was $66.431 billion in 2009, and the $12.220 billion output associated with defense spending accounted for 18.4 percent of the economy. However, our sensitivity analysis below suggests that these estimates may be high by about 10 percent, and we are aware that data limitations (e.g., accuracy of the adjusted consumption profile for defense personnel, accuracy of procurement data based on Hawaii as the principal place of performance) may affect the results.

The last three rows of Table 4.1 show the average multipliers for these expenditures, i.e., the ratios between total output, earnings, and employment in Hawaii and each category of defense spending. The output multiplier was 1.83 for earnings, 1.95 for procurement, and 1.87 overall. That is, each dollar of defense spending was associated with 87 cents of output in addition to the dollar of direct expenditure. The final-demand earnings multipliers are 0.48 for earnings, 0.63 for procurement, and 0.54 overall—each dollar of defense is associated with 54 cents of earnings in Hawaii through its effects on the economy. These earnings are in addition to the earnings of defense personnel. The employment multipliers show the number of full-time equivalent (FTE) jobs in Hawaii per million dollars of expenditure. The employment multiplier is 16.13 for earnings, 17.16 for procurement, and 16.52 overall. Each $1 million of defense spending was associated with 16.52 FTE jobs in Hawaii's economy.

Although the input-output model can provide a good assessment of the relationship between defense spending and output, earnings, and employment, we caution against using it to estimate the effects of a given increase or decrease in defense spending on the economy. As suggested above, an analysis of such a change should be based on a detailed structural model of the industries affected by the change, which we realize is not always practicable. Still, our caution means that, say, a $1 increase in defense spending will not necessarily result in an increase in output of $1.87.

Table 4.2 lists the 15 industry classes with the largest final-demand output effects. The table shows the output, earnings, and employment impacts of each industry class. Tables for

---

8   Expenditures in Table 4.1 are in 2009 dollars. However, the input-output model uses 2006 dollars, and accurate computation of employment requires that expenditures also be calculated in 2006 dollars. This has been done.

Table 4.2
Top 15 Industry Classes Ranked by Final-Demand Output

Industry Class	Final-Demand Output ($ thousands)	Final-Demand Earnings ($ thousands)	Final-Demand Employment (jobs)
7. Construction	1,593,140	529,367	13,841
47. Professional, scientific, and technical services	1,119,514	399,707	10,267
28. Retail trade	1,089,471	334,283	12,609
45. Real estate	835,548	124,499	4,633
59. Other services	619,189	175,308	6,160
58. Food services and drinking places	546,672	150,103	7,355
19. Food, beverage, and tobacco product manufacturing	508,195	103,782	3,149
27. Wholesale trade	459,688	142,477	3,648
49. Administrative and support services	440,584	153,956	5,892
52. Ambulatory healthcare services	398,763	147,475	3,641
24. Petroleum and coal products manufacturing	389,374	60,192	975
43. Insurance carriers and related activities	337,329	92,426	2,245
53. Hospitals and nursing and residential care facilities	311,348	109,833	2,976
51. Educational services	296,716	105,262	4,066
6. Utilities	280,951	50,667	942
Total of top 15 industry classes	9,226,482	2,679,336	82,399
Total of all industry classes	12,219,680	3,506,276	101,532

the earnings and employment rankings have been omitted because they are similar to the output rankings. For instance, 13 of the top 15 industries by output are among the top 15 industries by employment. These industries account for 75 percent of the total impact on output, earnings, and employment.

The RIMS II model contains multipliers for each of the 60 industrial classes, and the average multiplier for this analysis depends on how the defense expenditures are distributed over the classes. If the allocation of expenditures across industrial classes were to change in future years, the average multiplier would differ. Separate tables in Appendix D provide detailed information on the allocation of adjusted earnings by industry class, adjusted procurement expenditures by industry class, and their sum by industry class. The tables also present the multipliers by class and the output, earnings, and employment estimates by class.

Sensitivity Analysis

We next considered how the estimates might change as a result of data limitations or from the inclusion or exclusion of specific items, including undercounting or overcounting of defense procurement, Hawaii state taxes paid by defense personnel, personnel savings rate, Impact Aid to schools in Hawaii, spending by afloat and deployed personnel, and procurement by commissaries and exchanges. We also made a rough estimate of the portion of employment going to military spouses.

Use of the Hawaii input-output model implicitly assumes that the relationships and multipliers of the model are relevant to defense spending. But if defense expenditures for procurement and personnel were more likely to flow out of Hawaii to the mainland than equivalent-size non-defense expenditures, the model would produce overestimates. If this "leakage" meant that defense expenditures were in effect 10 percent less, for example, the output, earnings, and employment impacts would be 10 percent less. This calculation is straightforward, because the model is linear. Working in the other direction, our procurement data do not include contracts to companies that are based on the mainland and have the mainland as the principal place of performance but supply services and goods to defense agencies in Hawaii. If this inflow would in effect increase defense expenditures relevant to Hawaii, the output, earnings, and employment estimates would increase. Available data do not identify the leakage or inflow, however, so we do not offer specific estimates.

We estimated Hawaii state taxes paid by defense personnel to be $113 million (Table 2.2). This amount was excluded from total defense spending in Table 4.1; including it would increase defense spending by 1.7 percent and increase output, earnings, and employment by roughly the same percentage.

We do not know the savings rate of defense personnel and have assumed a zero rate. If the rate were, say, 4 percent, the impacts of personnel expenditures would decrease by 4 percent.[9] Personnel expenditures constitute 62 percent of total expenditures in Table 4.1, so the overall impact would be to decrease output, earnings, and employment by about 2.5 percent.

Our defense procurement numbers did not include DoD Impact Aid to Hawaii schools.[10] If Hawaii's $37 million in basic support under this program were included as a DoD expenditure and allocated to the industry class for education services, the overall estimates in Table 4.1 would show an additional $80 million in output (0.6 percent higher), $28 million higher earnings, and 1,092 higher employment.[11]

Afloat personnel may also affect the estimates. As noted in Chapter Two, there were an estimated 5,600 afloat personnel among the roughly 48,000 active-duty personnel in 2007–2009. If afloat personnel spend more of their military pay outside of Hawaii, the estimates in Table 4.1 are too high. To adjust for this, we can assume that afloat personnel are at sea for six months of each year and spend none of their at-sea earnings in Hawaii. Equivalently, we could assume that afloat personnel are at sea throughout most of the year but spend half of their at-sea earnings in Hawaii. Either assumption would decrease total after-tax personnel expenditures available for Hawaii by about 4 percent and total overall defense expenditures by

---

[9] Military personnel with 10 or more years of service are likely to stay in the military until at least 20 years of service, at which time they qualify for military retirement benefits. The military has a defined benefit plan with no contributions from service members. Thus, for service members expecting to qualify for retirement benefits, the expected value of those benefits can be construed as a form of savings. Although percentages vary somewhat over time, in 2000, about 18 percent of active-duty personnel could expect to qualify for nondisability retirement. Most service members do not qualify for military retirement benefits and may therefore have a stronger incentive to save than those who qualify. According to the DoD Office of the Actuary, "Based on current decrement rates, 18 percent of a typical group of new entrants attain 20 years of active duty service and become eligible for nondisability retirement from active duty. Specifically, 46 percent of new officers and 16 percent of new enlistees attain 20 years of active duty service" (U.S. Department of Defense, 2000).

[10] Impact Aid compensates local education agencies that have higher enrollment of federally connected children, including those of military personnel, and for the presence of tax-exempt federal property, including military installations. Impact Aid funds are general-purpose funds. The 2009 budget allocated a total of $1.128 billion for these purposes (basic support payments) and $48 million for children with disabilities. Hawaii received basic support of $37 million in 2008 and $36 million in 2009 (U.S. Department of Education, 2009).

[11] The multipliers for education are high, which accounts for the relatively large size of these increases. The multipliers are 2.15 for output, 0.76 for earnings, and 29.5 for employment.

about 2.6 percent.[12] But Navy personnel may save much of their at-sea money and spend it in Hawaii when they return, or dependents residing in Hawaii may spend it during their absence.

Similar points apply to deployed personnel in the Army, Air Force, and Marine Corps, e.g., personnel serving in Iraq, Afghanistan, or areas near those countries. Soldiers and Marines have been heavily deployed, and in 2007 and 2008, soldiers had been deployed an average of 12 months in a 36-month period, or one-third of the time (Hosek and Martorell, 2009; Bonds et al., 2010). Air Force deployments were typically shorter, averaging 3 to 4 months, compared with 7 months for Marine Corps deployments and 12 months or more for Army deployments. If we assumed that soldiers and Marines were deployed one-third of the time and airmen one-sixth of the time, and further assumed that half of their earnings when deployed were spent in Hawaii and all earnings when not deployed were spent in Hawaii, the personnel expenditure in Table 4.1 would decrease by $266 million.[13] If we include afloat personnel, the decrease would be $441 million. This is 10.8 percent of adjusted personnel expenditures and 6.8 percent of adjusted total expenditures.

Sensitivity estimates may also be made by industry class, using the tables in Appendix D, which contain the output, earnings, and employment multipliers by industry. For example, these tables could be used to show how a change in the mix of procurement expenditures would change the results.

Another issue is the question of whether the estimates are sensitive to how procurement by commissaries and exchanges is handled. As shown in Chapter Three, Defense Commissary Agency procurement totaled $45 million. However, apart from any appropriated-fund DoD civilians employed by the commissaries and exchanges, which we counted among DoD civilian employees, we treated commissaries and exchanges as a part of Hawaii's economy. Defense personnel can spend their earnings on goods and services from retailers throughout Hawaii, including commissaries and exchanges. Spending at commissaries and exchanges induces them to make purchases from vendors and employ workers, just like other retail outlets. The model provides estimates of the overall impact of this demand, but in the case of commissaries and exchanges, including Commissary Agency procurement may be double-counting. If the $45 million were excluded, the overall procurement would be associated with approximately $88 million less in output (0.7 percent), $28 million less in earnings, and 770 fewer jobs.

Finally, as a different sensitivity calculation, we estimated approximately how much of the overall employment impact in Hawaii consists of military spouses. Military spouses who work or seek work are part of Hawaii's labor force, so it is expected that they would hold some of the jobs. We estimate that they hold perhaps 5,000 of the 105,533 jobs associated with defense spending.[14]

---

[12] The 5,600 afloat personnel comprise 39 percent of the 14,237 Navy personnel, and we assumed they had that percentage of Navy earnings. Navy after-tax earnings were $0.876 billion, so half of afloat earnings were $0.172 billion. If this amount was not spent in Hawaii, it would decrease total adjusted after-tax personnel expenditures by 4.2 percent. Adjusted personnel expenditures are 62 percent of total expenditures in Table 4.1, so total expenditures would decrease by 2.6 percent (4.2×0.62).

[13] Details available upon request.

[14] There are approximately 55,000 dependents of active-duty military personnel in Hawaii (State of Hawaii, "State of Hawaii Data Book," 2009). Suppose there are 35,000 military spouses and assume they are not service members. The labor-force participation rate of military spouses is about 70 percent (Hosek et al., 2002), implying that there are perhaps 25,000 working spouses. Employment in Hawaii numbered 627,000 in 2008, which suggests that working military spouses made up 4 percent of the labor force (25,000/627,000). Overall employment associated with DoD spending was 105,533 FTE

Summary

The RIMS II input-output model for Hawaii provides a consistent framework linking together the industry classes of the economy and end-user demand. The model is useful for showing the relationship between defense spending and output, earnings, and employment in Hawaii's economy.

We adjusted the data on defense personnel and procurement expenditures described in Chapters Two and Three and used them along with the multipliers of the Hawaii input-output model to estimate how much of Hawaii's output, earnings, and employment are attributable to defense spending. We found that the average annual defense expenditures in 2007–2009 of $6.527 billion (2009 dollars) were associated with $12.220 billion worth of output, $3.506 billion of earnings, and 101,533 jobs. The $12.220 billion in output was 18.4 percent of Hawaii's GDP of $64 billion in 2009. The 101,533 jobs were 16.5 percent of Hawaii's average employment of 612,550 (State of Hawaii, "State of Hawaii Data Book," 2009, Table 12.06). However, sensitivity estimates suggest that these amounts may be high.

We considered how the estimates would change in response to further possible adjustments, including overestimating or underestimating defense procurement (ambiguous impact on estimates), adding Hawaii state taxes paid by defense personnel (1.7 percent increase in output), subtracting personnel savings (decrease depending on savings rate, of perhaps 2.5 percent), adding Impact Aid to Hawaii schools (0.6 percent increase), adjusting for spending in Hawaii by afloat and deployed personnel (possible decrease of 7 percent), and subtracting procurement by commissaries and exchanges (0.7 percent decrease). Although we do not have specific information on several of these items, the output, earnings, and employment estimates are sensitive to the savings rate of defense personnel and to where the earnings of afloat and deployed personnel are spent. Our crude estimates suggest that these adjustments could decrease the overall results by about 10 percent.

---

jobs, or about 20 percent of Hawaii's 517,000 full-time workers in 2008. So perhaps 20 percent of the jobs held by the 25,000 working spouses, about 5,000 jobs, were associated with defense spending.

CHAPTER FIVE

Conclusions

This study has attempted to determine the impacts of defense expenditures on Hawaii's economy. We estimated annual average defense expenditures, after adjustments, of $6.527 billion in FY 2007–2009 (2009 dollars) and found that they accounted for economywide output of $12.220 billion, or 18.4 percent of Hawaii's 2009 GDP, along with $3.506 billion in earnings and 101,533 jobs. Further adjustments suggest that the actual amounts might be about 10 percent lower, depending on the savings rate of personnel and where personnel who are afloat or deployed spend their money. Also, the input-output model parameters may not be fully accurate for defense spending, which implies some uncertainty in the estimates.

In making our estimates, we distinguished between military activities per se and the contribution of defense spending to Hawaii's economy. We treated the earnings of defense personnel and the benefits received by military retirees as being available to be spent in Hawaii. We included only procurements in which Hawaii was the principal place of performance. Our estimates do not count the "jobs" of active-duty service members, DoD appropriated-fund civilian employees, and reservists; the personnel and material cost of healthcare provided at military treatment facilities; or the defense equipment and materiel purchased by DoD under contracts where Hawaii is not designated as the principal place of performance and shipped to Hawaii.

During the study, we spoke with officers and DoD civilian officials in the Army, Navy, Air Force, and Marine Corps, and at U.S. Pacific Command.[1] Their insights helped to inform our understanding of the data and recognize its strengths and limitations. The officials with whom we met indicated instances where the data might be incomplete, e.g., when officers and experts come to Hawaii for meetings and their travel expenses are paid from accounts at their home stations, or when an umbrella contract is let to a mainland firm that supplies communications services to installations in Hawaii. The database we developed is comprehensive within its collection parameters, reproducible, and based on government records on procurement and personnel. The input-output model is maintained and updated by BEA and adapted to Hawaii. The databases and BEA's ongoing support for the input-output model mean that similar analyses can be done in the future. Resolving some of the data limitations, however, will require original data collection and analysis.

We think it likely that further refinement of the data and model will still reveal that defense spending is associated with considerable economic activity in Hawaii. As noted in Chapters Two and Three, defense procurement in Hawaii has increased twofold, by $1 billion since the mid-1990s, and the number of defense personnel (excluding reservists and afloat personnel), which had been between 55,000 and 57,700 since the mid-1990s, has increased

---

[1] U.S. Pacific Command is one of six unified combatant commands of the U.S. armed forces.

since 2007 to about 60,000. Public interest groups, government, and businesses may be interested in the effects of this increase on the dynamics of Hawaii's economy, perhaps leading to investments in Hawaii's private sector, infrastructure, and people. We hope that this study will contribute to their discussions.

Data Sources and Analysis

This appendix describes the data sources and data selection criteria and assumptions made in assembling our summary information on military personnel and procurements in Hawaii.

Military Personnel Data

We used data from DMDC for earnings and demographic information on active-duty, Reserve, and DoD civilian employee populations based in or living in Hawaii in FY 2007–2009.

Active-Duty Population

Data on the active-duty population in Hawaii were obtained from DMDC's Active Duty Master File (demographic information) and Active Duty Pay File (earnings information). Information was reported quarterly for all those with a duty state of Hawaii during the quarter, including those who had been deployed.[1] Reservists serving on active duty were counted as part of the active-duty population.

Demographic information on family income was obtained by combining DMDC data with information from the ACS (2006–2008, three-year sample) using the *Integrated Public Use Microdata Series* (Ruggles et al., 2010). Active-duty service members were identified in the ACS as those with an employment status of "active duty."[2] The sample size for active-duty service members in the ACS data is 988 individuals.

Reserve Population

Data on the Reserve population in Hawaii were collected from DMDC's Reserve Components Common Personnel Data System (demographic information) and the Reserve Pay File (earnings information). Information was reported quarterly for Reserve and National Guard members who had a duty state of Hawaii during the relevant period. Reservists serving on active duty were not included here, as they were grouped with the active-duty population.

DoD Civilian Employee Population

Data on DoD appropriated-fund civilian employees in Hawaii were collected from DMDC's Civilian Personnel file and Civilian Pay file. Information was reported quarterly.

---

[1] The duty state was Hawaii unless the individual was permanently assigned elsewhere.

[2] The ACS asks, "For whom did this person work? If now on active duty in the armed forces, mark (X) in this box and print the branch of the Armed Forces."

Veterans and Retirees

Characteristics and earnings of the veteran and retiree population in Hawaii were estimated using ACS data (Ruggles et al., 2010) and State of Hawaii, "State of Hawaii Data Book," 2007, 2008, 2009, Table 10.29.

Demographic Estimates for the Population of Hawaii

We used demographic and earnings information for the population of Hawaii for comparisons with defense personnel. The comparisons provided background information and were not used in the input-output analysis. The data were from the ACS (Ruggles et al., 2010), which generates a representative sample of individuals. All of the individuals in this sample ages 17 and older and living in the state of Hawaii were included in the analysis, with the exception of those serving on active duty. However, we based our earnings tabulations on full-time workers and our family-income tabulations on families with a full-time worker ages 17 and older, again excluding those on active duty. Full-time workers include individuals doing paid work for at least 35 hours a week and 40 weeks a year. We describe below how we estimated family income for families with a member serving on active duty and compared it with the income of families without a member serving on active duty.

Assumptions and Estimations Used in Compiling Personnel Data

We obtained most of our earnings information from DMDC in quarterly datasets that reported a value for the previous month's earnings. Quarterly earnings were estimated by multiplying the reported monthly earnings by three. Annual earnings were then calculated by summing the estimated quarterly earnings. This process does not require the individual to reside in Hawaii for the entire year; rather, in effect, it estimates earnings for the active-duty, Reserve, and DoD civilian positions in Hawaii. The positions are nearly always filled, and their number is approximately constant during a quarter, although different individuals may fill some positions as some depart and others arrive. This method will overestimate the earnings of reservists if they are on their 12 to 14 days of active-duty training in the last month of a quarter. Even so, Reserve earnings were only 4 percent of total earnings of defense personnel, so the overestimate seems negligible.

Active-duty earnings consist of basic pay, special and incentive pays, a cost-of-living allowance, and tax-exempt allowances for housing and subsistence.[3] These allowances make up roughly one-third of total active-duty earnings, generating additional value for the service member because they are tax-exempt. For demographic comparisons, the tax advantage was quantified by subtracting estimated taxes on family income (see below) without these allowances from estimated taxes on income including these allowances. In these calculations, we assumed that active-duty service members paid Hawaii state tax. This is likely to be an overestimate, because a service member's state of residence for tax purposes may be elsewhere and chosen because it has low or zero state income tax. This tax advantage was added to individual earnings and family income.

Reservist earnings consist primarily of basic pay but can also include a Reserve housing allowance (when on active-duty training), bonus payments, and special and incentive payments.

---

[3] Military families also have access to subsidized childcare. This was not included.

Overseas cost of living allowances (OCOLAs) for active-duty service members were estimated. Rates were determined using an OCOLA calculator (Defense Travel Management Office, "Overseas COLA Calculator," undated), which requires information on year, location, pay grade, years of service, and number of dependents. To simplify this process, individuals were aggregated by year, pay grade, and marital status. For each pay grade, the mode of years of service was determined using the DMDC data on active-duty service members. Married individuals were assumed to have two dependents, and unmarried individuals, zero dependents. We assumed that all individuals were based in Oahu. Individuals living in barracks receive a lower rate of OCOLA; we used data from Hickam Air Force Base (2008) to estimate the fraction of unmarried individuals living in barracks.

We calculated estimates of family income for active-duty service members, using a combination of DMDC and ACS data. For this population, self-reported earnings from the ACS are substantially lower than the military earnings estimated from DMDC data. This may be because individuals do not always include allowances such as the Basic Allowance for Housing and the Basic Allowance for Subsistence. We therefore used individual earnings from DMDC data to measure the earnings of the military member.

We estimated additional family income from the ACS data by subtracting self-reported member earnings from family income. To estimate total family income, the mean and median of additional family income from the ACS data were added to the mean and median individual earnings from the DMDC data.

The estimates of taxes paid were based on withheld-tax variables in the datasets when available. Withheld taxes may not be a true reflection of final tax amount paid, however. When tax information was unavailable in the data, it was estimated. For example, tax data for DoD civilians were not available in the DMDC data. Also unavailable for this group was tax-relevant information on marital status and number of dependents. For each DoD civilian, marital status and number of dependents were simulated on the basis of income and demographic characteristics of the population of Hawaii, as represented in ACS data. Federal and Hawaii state taxes were estimated using these simulated demographic characteristics and known income. Assuming the DoD civilian population is demographically similar to the population at large, given income, this should generate a tax estimate that is reasonably accurate in aggregate. FICA taxes were estimated for all groups based on income.

Procurement Data

Procurement data were extracted from the Federal Procurement Data System, a publicly accessible database of U.S. government procurements managed by the Federal Procurement Data Center that includes contracts greater than $3,000,[4] including all contract modifications (Federal Procurement Data System, undated). It does not include contracts that primarily use nonappropriated funds.

The Federal Procurement Data System database includes variables such as the contracting government agency, the contract amount, some vendor characteristics such as vendor name and location, and the type of good or service purchased.

---

[4] Contracts of less than $3,000 are not included in the data, which will cause an underestimate of military spending.

Data were selected that met three criteria:

1. defense spending
2. in Hawaii
3. in FY 2007–2009.

Defense spending was identified through the contracting-agency variable. Data were included if they were associated with the seven military-related agencies that had significant annual procurements, i.e., the Department of the Navy, Department of the Army, Department of the Air Force, Defense Logistics Agency, Defense Information Systems Agency, Defense Commissary Agency, and U.S. Coast Guard. Approximately 3 percent of the value of DoD Hawaii procurements is associated with other agencies and is not included.

We used the principal place of performance to identify goods and services that were used ("performed") primarily in Hawaii.

There are four possible combinations of contract with respect to Hawaii and the U.S. mainland, including Alaska:

- Contractor location is Hawaii and the principal place of performance is Hawaii. We included this category in our study, as we are confident that nearly all funds spent in such a contract will be for consumption of goods and services in Hawaii's economy.
- Contractor location is the mainland and the principal place of performance is Hawaii. We included this category, assuming that the vast majority of funds spent on such a contract would be for consumption of goods and services in Hawaii's economy. Including such contracts may overestimate the quantity of goods and services demanded from Hawaii's economy. Since the contractor is located on the mainland, it is likely that management functions and some support functions are performed in an office there. The portion of expenses in the contract that compensate the contractor for these services will be spent in rent, operations costs, and pay to employees on the mainland.
- Contractor location is Hawaii and the principal place of performance is the mainland. We excluded this category of contract, although that may underestimate the quantity of activity DoD contributed to Hawaii's economy. Contractors located in Hawaii are likely to procure goods and services in Hawaii to provide management and support services to the contractor division that performs the contracted work on the mainland. Excluding this category of contract excludes this potential activity in Hawaii's economy.
- Contractor location is the mainland and the principal place of performance is the mainland. We excluded this type of contract and therefore may have underestimated the DoD activity in Hawaii's economy. For example, a DoD-wide contract to a mainland contractor to provide computing support services to all military installations has its principal place of performance on the mainland. However, the mainland contractor may hire staff in Hawaii either directly or through a subcontract to perform services at military installations in Hawaii. By excluding this type of contract, we may have omitted such contributions to Hawaii's economy. TRICARE contracts are an example of this, but we obtained estimates from TRICARE of healthcare spending for civilian providers who care for dependents and retirees.

In sum, we included contracts in which Hawaii is the principal place of performance regardless of whether the vendor has a Hawaii address or not. This approach will overestimate the economic contribution to Hawaii if a portion of the economic activity takes place elsewhere. Conversely, the economic contributions of contracts with a principal place of performance outside of Hawaii will be underestimated if a portion of the economic activity takes place in Hawaii. As a limited test of this approach, we found that it has good coverage of procurement contracts for vendors based in Hawaii: 95 percent of the goods and services (by value) provided by Hawaii-based vendors have Hawaii as the principal place of performance. Thus, although this approach provides only an estimate of the procurement value within Hawaii, we believe it to be a reasonable one.

Procurements were selected that had a contract date during FY 2007–2009. Data for earlier years had substantial gaps.

Once the relevant procurements were identified, they were classified into the 60 Aggregated Industry Codes used by the model. This was done using the variables "NAICS code," "NAICS description," and "product or service description."

Comparison of Military Personnel and the Population in Hawaii

We compared the education, individual earnings, and family income of defense personnel with those of Hawaii's population ages 17 and older, using DMDC and ACS data.

Education

Figure B.1 shows educational attainment of active-duty personnel in Hawaii in 2009, about 85 percent of whom were enlisted and 15 percent were officers. The vast majority of enlisted personnel (86 percent) had a high school diploma; less than 1 percent had less than a high school education, and 13 percent had some college or a college degree. Among officers, 54 percent had a four-year college degree, and 42 percent had some post-graduate education. The high percentage (73 percent) of active-duty personnel with high school as their highest level of education reflects the fact that 85 percent of active-duty personnel were enlisted.

Figure B.1
Educational Attainment of Active-Duty Personnel

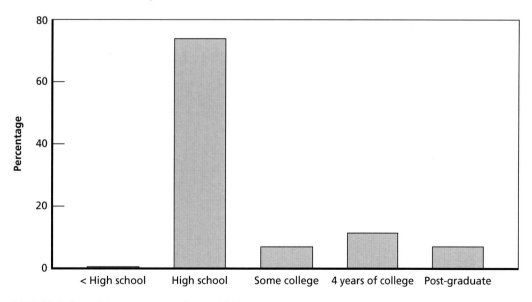

SOURCE: Defense Manpower Data Center, 2009.
RAND *TR996-B.1*

35

Figure B.2 shows educational attainment of Hawaii's population ages 17 and older, excluding individuals serving on active duty. (The scale of this figure differs from that of Figure B.1.) Ten percent did not graduate from high school, 38 percent had a high school diploma, 25 percent had some college, more than 17 percent had a four-year college degree, and more than 8 percent had post-graduate education. That is, 26 percent had four or more years of college.

DoD civilians had relatively high educational attainment compared with the population in Hawaii: 35 percent of the DoD civilians had a four-year college degree or higher, and only 1 percent did not have a high school diploma (Figure B.3). The educational attainment of National Guard and Reserve members (not shown) was like that of DoD civilians, but with slightly lower college levels (29 percent had a four-year college degree or more; 28 percent had some college).

How Do Military Earnings Compare with Those of Hawaii's Full-Time Civilian Workers?

Active-duty members and DoD civilian employees earned more on average than Hawaii's full-time workers. However, the difference in earnings that are apparent from a comparison of DoD personnel earnings with those of Hawaii full-time workers diminish substantially when we compare the incomes of families that have a full-time worker. Figures B.4 and B.5 show the earnings distributions for active-duty service members and DoD civilian employees for FY 2007–2009 in 2009 dollars. Figure B.6 shows the earnings distribution of full-time workers ages 17 and older. Table B.1 provides estimates of the median and mean individual earnings (first two rows) and family income (second two rows) for active-duty personnel, Hawaii full-time workers ages 17 and older, and Hawaii full-time workers ages 17 to 50.

Figure B.2
Educational Attainment of Population of Hawaii, Ages 17 and Older

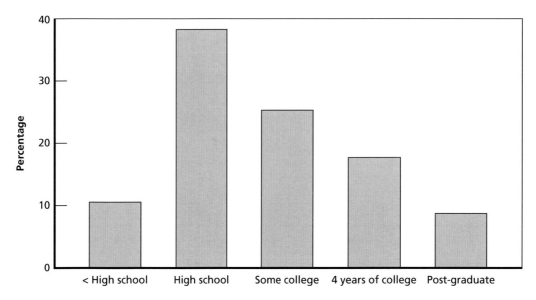

SOURCE: Authors' tabulations from data in U.S. Census Bureau, undated.
RAND *TR996-B.2*

Figure B.3
Educational Attainment of DoD Civilians

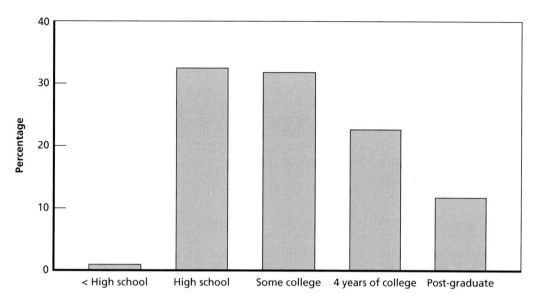

SOURCE: Authors' tabulations from data in Defense Manpower Data Center, 2009.
RAND *TR996-B.3*

Figure B.4
Annual Pay of Active-Duty Service Members, 2007–2009

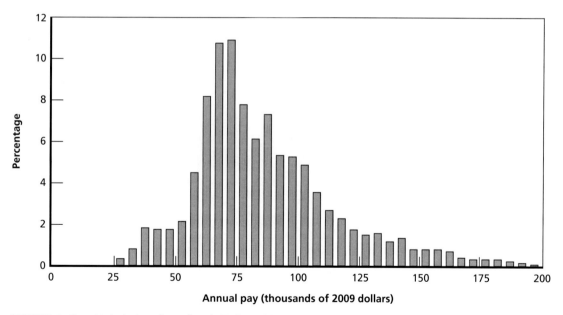

SOURCE: Authors' tabulations from data in Defense Manpower Data Center, 2009.
RAND *TR996-B.4*

Figure B.5
Annual Pay of DoD Civilian Employees

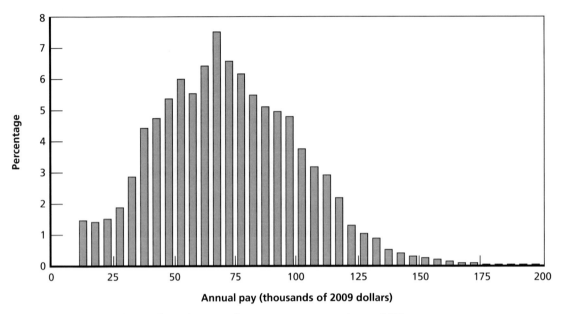

SOURCE: Authors' tabulations from data in Defense Manpower Data Center, 2009.
RAND *TR996-B.5*

Figure B.6
Annual Pay of Full-Time Workers in Hawaii, Ages 17 and Older

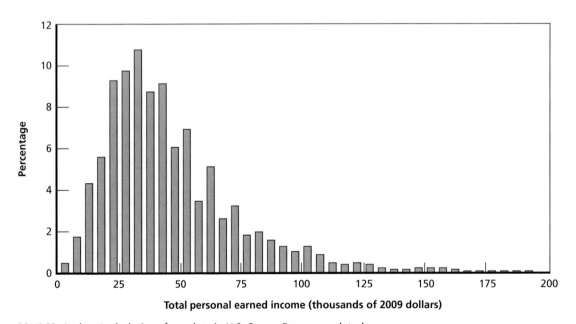

SOURCE: Authors' tabulations from data in U.S. Census Bureau, undated.
RAND *TR996-B.6*

As seen in Table B.1, active-duty personnel had median annual earnings of $74,871. (Enlisted and officer earnings differ, with enlisted personnel having median earnings of $70,780 and officers having median earnings of $127,564. Also, DoD appropriated-fund civilians had median earnings of $69,832.) Full-time workers ages 17 and older had median earnings of $40,000, and those of workers ages 17 to 50 were $37,383.

The entries in Table B.1 for family income are relevant because the consumer unit is typically the family.[1] Family income in Hawaii is much higher than individual earnings, reflecting the presence of multiple workers plus income other than wages. Active-duty family income is only slightly higher than the earnings of active-duty service members, because of lower employment and wages of active-duty spouses (Harrell et al., 2004; Hosek et al., 2002). Our estimate of median family income for active-duty personnel is $87,298, which compares with median family incomes of $85,003 for families with a full-time worker ages 17 or older and $80,478 for families with a full-time worker ages 17 to 50.

Further, although not shown, the earnings of National Guard members and reservists—both deployed and non-deployed—in their capacity as service members averaged $20,135 per year.

Table B.1
Individual Earnings and Family Income (thousands of 2009 dollars)

	Active-Duty Personnel	Hawaii Full-Time Workers Ages 17+	Hawaii Full-Time Workers Ages 17–50
Median earnings	74,871	40,000	37,383
Average earnings	80,155	50,436	45,955
Median family income	87,298	85,003	80,478
Average family income	94,369	102,093	95,128

SOURCE: Authors' tabulations, DMDC data for 2007–2009 and ACS data for 2006–2008 (Ruggles et al., 2010). The estimates for Hawaii full-time workers exclude active-duty personnel.

---

[1] Like the earnings estimates, the family income estimates are for families with a full-time worker.

The Bureau of Economic Analysis Regional Input-Output Model

We applied our adjusted defense expenditure data to the model and used RIMS II "final demand" multipliers for the state of Hawaii based on data from 2006. Final-demand multipliers capture the direct and indirect effect of purchases.

BEA modifies the national input-output model as follows to obtain its regional model (U.S. Department of Commerce, undated):

> The RIMS II method for estimating regional I-O [input-output] multipliers can be viewed as a three step process. In the first step, the producer portion of the national I-O table is made region-specific by using six-digit NAICS location quotients (LQs). The LQs estimate the extent to which input requirements are supplied by firms within the region. RIMS II uses LQs based on two types of data: BEA's personal income data (by place of residence) are used to calculate LQs in the service industries; and BEA's wage-and-salary data (by place of work) are used to calculate LQs in the nonservice industries.
>
> In the second step, the household row and the household column from the national I-O table are made region-specific. The household row coefficients, which are derived from the value-added row of the national I-O table, are adjusted to reflect regional earnings leakages resulting from individuals working in the region but residing outside the region. The household column coefficients, which are based on the personal consumption expenditure column of the national I-O table, are adjusted to account for regional consumption leakages stemming from personal taxes and savings.
>
> In the last step, the Leontief inversion approach is used to estimate multipliers. This inversion approach produces output, earnings, and employment multipliers, which can be used to trace the impacts of changes in final demand on directly and indirectly affected industries.

The Leontief inversion approach to which BEA refers is the input-output approach to modeling an economy created by Wassily Leontief. The basic input-output model can be described as follows. Let A = input-output matrix, x = total output vector, c = final demand vector, and I = identity matrix. Then total output can be written as a function of final demand as follows:

$$Ax + c = x$$
$$(I - A)x = c$$
$$x = (I - A)^{-1}c .$$

In our application to Hawaii, c can represent the final demand for produced goods and services resulting from defense procurement expenditures. Similarly, recalling that the input-output matrix includes a household row and column and therefore allows for consumption effects, c can also represent the consumption associated with defense personnel expenditures.

BEA applies the LQs as follows to obtain the regional input-output matrix:

> If the LQ for a row industry in the regional direct requirements table is greater than, or equal to, one, it is assumed that the region's demand for the output of the row industry is met entirely from regional production. In this instance, all row entries for the industry in the regional direct requirements table are set equal to the corresponding entries in the adjusted national direct requirements table.

> Conversely, if the LQ is less than one, it is assumed that regional supply of the industry's output is not sufficient to meet regional demand. In this instance, all row entries for the industry in the regional direct requirements table are set equal to the product of the corresponding entries in the adjusted national direct requirements table and the LQ for the industry.

> The household row and the household column that were added to the national direct requirements table are also adjusted regionally.

The household-row entries are adjusted downward, on the basis of commuting data from the Census of Population and Housing (U.S. Census Bureau, undated), to account for the purchases made outside the region by commuters working in the region. The household-column entries are adjusted downward, on the basis of tax data from the Internal Revenue Service, to account for the dampening effect of state and local taxes on household expenditures (U.S. Department of Commerce, 1997, p. 23).

Tables for Final-Demand Output, Earnings, and Employment Associated with Defense Spending in Hawaii

Tables D.1, D.2, and D.3 present the following information:

- Column 1: Adjusted defense expenditures for personnel allocated to industry class on the basis of Hawaii consumption (final demand) expenditure allocations (Table D.1); adjusted defense expenditures for procurement allocated to industry class based on the NAICS code on each defense contractor's record (Table D.2); and adjusted defense expenditures for personnel and procurement (Table D.3).
- Columns 2–4: Final-demand output, earnings, and employment multipliers by industry class, as provided by RIMS II for Hawaii.
- Columns 5–7: Final-demand output, earnings, and employment impacts of defense spending, computed as the product of the entry in column 1 and the respective multiplier.

The defense expenditures in column 1 of Tables D.1, D.2, and D.3 are annual averages for 2007–2009 in 2006 dollars. The RIMS II Hawaii model is in 2006 dollars, so defense expenditures should be in 2006 dollars to provide a correct estimate of the employment effect. We converted 2009 dollars to 2006 dollars with a factor of 0.94195, the geometric average of GDP deflator changes between 2006 and 2009, quarter by quarter. To convert 2009 dollars to 2006 dollars, multiply by this factor; to convert 2006 dollars to 2009 dollars, multiply by 1.06163 (1/0.94195).

Table D.1
Earnings

	Revised Allocation (thousands of $2006)	Final-Demand Output ($)	Final-Demand Earnings ($)	Final-Demand Employment (jobs/$million)	Final-Demand Output ($thousands)	Final-Demand Earnings ($thousands)	Final-Demand Employment (jobs)
1. Crop and animal production	22,618	1.6138	0.3664	18.8842	36,500	8,287	427
2. Forestry, fishing, and related activities	3,350	1.9308	0.7354	34.9553	6,467	2,463	117
3. Oil and gas extraction	0	1	0	0	0	0	—
4. Mining, except oil and gas	112	1.6046	0.3692	7.4445	179	41	1
5. Support activities for mining	0	1.8761	0.4832	11.6551	0	0	—
6. Utilities	123,030	1.3369	0.2411	4.4824	164,478	29,662	551
7. Construction	0	2.0239	0.6725	17.5832	0	0	—
8. Wood product manufacturing	821	1.5761	0.3639	11.8473	1,294	299	10
9. Nonmetallic mineral product manufacturing	3,345	1.843	0.4447	10.3767	6,165	1,487	35
10. Primary metal manufacturing	501	1.3097	0.1679	3.6019	656	84	2
11. Fabricated metal product manufacturing	6,699	1.5478	0.3562	9.3663	10,368	2,386	63
12. Machinery manufacturing	4,276	1.5211	0.3384	9.4022	6,504	1,447	40
13. Computer and electronic product manufacturing	37,197	1.8516	0.6306	17.3905	68,873	23,456	647
14. Electrical equipment and appliance manufacturing	17,378	1.6644	0.4204	11.8733	28,924	7,306	206
15. Motor vehicle, body, trailer, and parts manufacturing	110,258	1.5815	0.3529	8.8123	174,373	38,910	972
16. Other transportation equipment manufacturing	10,241	1.7794	0.622	13.5249	18,222	6,370	139
17. Furniture and related product manufacturing	22,335	1.7311	0.4324	12.628	38,664	9,658	282
18. Miscellaneous manufacturing	44,407	1.7829	0.532	15.9414	79,173	23,624	708
19. Food, beverage, and tobacco product manufacturing	231,458	1.8828	0.3845	11.666	435,790	88,996	2,700
20. Textile and textile product mills	15,721	1.6715	0.4289	12.0428	26,277	6,743	189
21. Apparel, leather, and allied product manufacturing	68,732	1.8387	0.5998	27.0256	126,377	41,225	1,858
22. Paper manufacturing	10,056	1.6071	0.3567	8.6776	16,161	3,587	87
23. Printing and related support activities	1,517	1.7738	0.5417	16.4828	2,690	822	25
24. Petroleum and coal products manufacturing	105,140	1.3507	0.2088	3.3821	142,013	21,953	356
25. Chemical manufacturing	114,476	1.6249	0.3168	6.75	186,012	36,266	773
26. Plastics and rubber products manufacturing	13,096	1.5286	0.3211	9.1577	20,018	4,205	120
27. Wholesale trade	177,674	1.8397	0.5702	14.5997	326,868	101,310	2,594
28. Retail trade	503,473	1.9281	0.5916	22.3148	970,746	297,855	11,235
29. Air transportation	39,929	2.036	0.4955	13.3201	81,295	19,785	532
30. Rail transportation	3,778	1	0	0	3,778	0	—
31. Water transportation	7,146	2.1097	0.4502	12.3416	15,075	3,217	88

Table D.1—Continued

	Revised Allocation (thousands of $2006)	Final-Demand Output ($)	Final-Demand Earnings ($)	Final-Demand Employment (jobs/$million)	Final-Demand Output ($thousands)	Final-Demand Earnings ($thousands)	Final-Demand Employment (jobs)
32. Truck transportation	26,766	2.0269	0.5976	15.805	54,252	15,995	423
33. Transit and ground passenger transportation	11,167	2.1047	0.6995	40.9574	23,503	7,811	457
34. Pipeline transportation	369	1.7057	0.3055	6.2986	629	113	2
35. Other transportation and support activities	8,635	2.0235	0.7953	19.4377	17,473	6,867	168
36. Warehousing and storage	308	1.9659	0.7477	24.1407	605	230	7
37. Publishing including software	33,384	1.7848	0.4949	12.4276	59,584	16,522	415
38. Motion picture and sound recording industries	14,666	1.9458	0.4477	18.6018	28,537	6,566	273
39. Broadcasting and telecommunications	106,458	1.9822	0.3835	8.9783	211,021	40,827	956
40. Information and data processing services	11,958	1.9949	0.4971	14.0097	23,855	5,944	168
41. Federal Reserve banks, credit intermed., related services	125,549	1.6245	0.4483	11.241	203,954	56,283	1,411
42. Securities, commodity contracts, investments	52,266	2.0582	0.7422	24.2209	107,573	38,792	1,266
43. Insurance carriers and related activities	154,417	2.0526	0.5624	13.6606	316,957	86,844	2,109
44. Funds, trusts, and other financial vehicles	50,878	1.7423	0.4374	9.6151	88,645	22,254	489
45. Real estate	505,401	1.555	0.2317	8.6217	785,899	117,101	4,357
46. Rental/leasing services and lessors of intangible assets	32,751	2.1888	0.5105	16.4569	71,685	16,719	539
47. Professional, scientific, and technical services	76,958	2.0785	0.7421	19.061	159,957	57,111	1,467
48. Management of companies and enterprises	0	2.097	0.7024	14.7166	0	0	—
49. Administrative and support services	19,737	2.0679	0.7226	27.6549	40,815	14,262	546
50. Waste management and remediation services	7,225	2.0577	0.5468	14.1446	14,866	3,950	102
51. Educational services	112,867	2.1536	0.764	29.5122	243,069	86,230	3,331
52. Ambulatory healthcare services	28,054	2.0504	0.7583	18.7241	57,522	21,274	525
53. Hospitals and nursing and residential care facilities	28,054	2.1323	0.7522	20.3823	59,820	21,102	572
54. Social assistance	62,168	2.079	0.74	33.668	129,248	46,004	2,093
55. Performing arts, museums, and related activities	18,248	2.0669	0.7335	44.5509	37,718	13,385	813
56. Amusements, gambling, and recreation	75,065	1.881	0.5617	22.1301	141,196	42,164	1,661
57. Accommodation	58,048	1.8973	0.5547	18.3948	110,134	32,199	1,068
58. Food services and drinking places	256,306	1.9379	0.5321	26.0724	496,695	136,380	6,683
59. Other services	253,556	2.0408	0.5778	20.3042	517,457	146,505	5,148
60. Households	7,935	1.3174	0.3707	12.1654	10,453	2,941	97
Total	3,837,952				7,007,063	1,843,821	61,902
Average multiplier		1.83	0.48	16.13			

Table D.2
Procurement

	Revised Allocation (thousands of $2006)	Final-Demand Output ($)	Final-Demand Earnings ($)	Final-Demand Employment (jobs/$million)	Final-Demand Output ($thousands)	Final-Demand Earnings ($thousands)	Final-Demand Employment (jobs)
1. Crop and animal production	2,100	1.6138	0.3664	18.8842	3,389	770	40
2. Forestry, fishing, and related activities	127	1.9308	0.7354	34.9553	246	94	4
3. Oil and gas extraction	24	1	0.0000	0	24	0	—
4. Mining, except oil and gas	2,371	1.6046	0.3692	7.4445	3,804	875	18
5. Support activities for mining	4	1.8761	0.4832	11.6551	7	2	0
6. Utilities	74,922	1.3369	0.2411	4.4824	100,164	18,064	336
7. Construction	741,470	2.0239	0.6725	17.5832	1,500,661	498,639	13,037
8. Wood product manufacturing	150	1.5761	0.3639	11.8473	236	55	2
9. Nonmetallic mineral product manufacturing	433	1.843	0.4447	10.3767	799	193	4
10. Primary metal manufacturing	104	1.3097	0.1679	3.6019	136	17	0
11. Fabricated metal product manufacturing	5,087	1.5478	0.3562	9.3663	7,873	1,812	48
12. Machinery manufacturing	7,667	1.5211	0.3384	9.4022	11,663	2,595	72
13. Computer and electronic product manufacturing	21,552	1.8516	0.6306	17.3905	39,905	13,591	375
14. Electrical equipment and appliance manufacturing	4,332	1.6644	0.4204	11.8733	7,210	1,821	51
15. Motor vehicle, body, trailer, parts manufacturing	650	1.5815	0.3529	8.8123	1,027	229	6
16. Other transportation equipment manufacturing	84,956	1.7794	0.6220	13.5249	151,171	52,843	1,149
17. Furniture and related product manufacturing	12,257	1.7311	0.4324	12.628	21,218	5,300	155
18. Miscellaneous manufacturing	8,664	1.7829	0.5320	15.9414	15,447	4,609	138
19. Food, beverage, and tobacco product manufacturing	22,788	1.8828	0.3845	11.666	42,905	8,762	266
20. Textile and textile product mills	1,328	1.6715	0.4289	12.0428	2,221	570	16
21. Apparel, leather, and allied product manufacturing	1,093	1.8387	0.5998	27.0256	2,009	655	30
22. Paper manufacturing	170	1.6071	0.3567	8.6776	274	61	1
23. Printing and related support activities	211	1.7738	0.5417	16.4828	374	114	3
24. Petroleum and coal products manufacturing	166,402	1.3507	0.2088	3.3821	224,759	34,745	563
25. Chemical manufacturing	5,259	1.6249	0.3168	6.75	8,545	1,666	35
26. Plastics and rubber products manufacturing	480	1.5286	0.3211	9.1577	734	154	4
27. Wholesale trade	57,692	1.8397	0.5702	14.5997	106,136	32,896	842
28. Retail trade	28,776	1.9281	0.5916	22.3148	55,483	17,024	642
29. Air transportation	5,667	2.036	0.4955	13.3201	11,538	2,808	75
30. Rail transportation	0	1	0.0000	0	0	0	—
31. Water transportation	8,552	2.1097	0.4502	12.3416	18,043	3,850	106

Table D.2—Continued

	Revised Allocation (thousands of $2006)	Final-Demand Output ($)	Final-Demand Earnings ($)	Final-Demand Employment (jobs/$million)	Final-Demand Output ($thousands)	Final-Demand Earnings ($thousands)	Final-Demand Employment (jobs)
32. Truck transportation	1,680	2.0269	0.5976	15.805	3,404	1,004	27
33. Transit and ground passenger transportation	1,062	2.1047	0.6995	40.9574	2,235	743	44
34. Pipeline transportation	0	1.7057	0.3055	6.2986	0	0	—
35. Other transportation and support activities	23,429	2.0235	0.7953	19.4377	47,409	18,633	455
36. Warehousing and storage	5,984	1.9659	0.7477	24.1407	11,764	4,474	144
37. Publishing including software	1,380	1.7848	0.4949	12.4276	2,463	683	17
38. Motion picture and sound recording industries	56	1.9458	0.4477	18.6018	110	25	1
39. Broadcasting and telecommunications	1,209	1.9822	0.3835	8.9783	2,397	464	11
40. Information and data processing services	0	1.9949	0.4971	14.0097	0	0	—
41. Federal Reserve banks, credit intermed., and related services	30	1.6245	0.4483	11.241	49	14	0
42. Securities, commodity contracts, investments	7	2.0582	0.7422	24.2209	14	5	0
43. Insurance carriers and related activities	385	2.0526	0.5624	13.6606	791	217	5
44. Funds, trusts, and other financial vehicles	0	1.7423	0.4374	9.6151	0	0	—
45. Real estate	738	1.555	0.2317	8.6217	1,147	171	6
46. Rental and leasing services and lessors of intangible assets	5,232	2.1888	0.5105	16.4569	11,452	2,671	86
47. Professional, scientific, and technical services	430,392	2.0785	0.7421	19.061	894,570	319,394	8,204
48. Management of companies and enterprises	0	2.097	0.7024	14.7166	0	0	—
49. Administrative and support services	180,953	2.0679	0.7226	27.6549	374,194	130,757	5,004
50. Waste management and remediation services	62,764	2.0577	0.5468	14.1446	129,149	34,319	888
51. Educational services	16,913	2.1536	0.7640	29.5122	36,423	12,921	499
52. Ambulatory healthcare services	155,137	2.0504	0.7583	18.7241	318,093	117,640	2,905
53. Hospitals and nursing and residential care facilities	109,485	2.1323	0.7522	20.3823	233,455	82,355	2,232
54. Social assistance	1,574	2.079	0.7400	33.668	3,272	1,165	53
55. Performing arts, museums, and related activities	1,772	2.0669	0.7335	44.5509	3,663	1,300	79
56. Amusements, gambling, and recreation	4	1.881	0.5617	22.1301	8	3	0
57. Accommodation	2,735	1.8973	0.5547	18.3948	5,189	1,517	50
58. Food services and drinking places	9,414	1.9379	0.5321	26.0724	18,243	5,009	245
59. Other services	32,237	2.0408	0.5778	20.3042	65,790	18,627	655
60. Households	0	1.3174	0.3707	12.1654	0	0	—
Total	2,309,861				4,503,284	1,458,921	39,631

Table D.3
Total Defense Spending

	Revised Allocation (thousands of $2006)	Final-Demand Output ($)	Final-Demand Earnings ($)	Final-Demand Employment (jobs/$million)	Final-Demand Output ($thousands)	Final-Demand Earnings ($thousands)	Final-Demand Employment (jobs)
1. Crop and animal production	24,718	1.6138	0.3664	18.8842	39,890	9,057	467
2. Forestry, fishing, and related activities	3,477	1.9308	0.7354	34.9553	6,713	2,557	122
3. Oil and gas extraction	24	1	0.0000	0	24	0	—
4. Mining, except oil and gas	2,482	1.6046	0.3692	7.4445	3,983	916	18
5. Support activities for mining	4	1.8761	0.4832	11.6551	7	2	0
6. Utilities	197,952	1.3369	0.2411	4.4824	264,642	47,726	887
7. Construction	741,470	2.0239	0.6725	17.5832	1,500,661	498,639	13,037
8. Wood product manufacturing	971	1.5761	0.3639	11.8473	1,530	353	11
9. Nonmetallic mineral product manufacturing	3,778	1.843	0.4447	10.3767	6,963	1,680	39
10. Primary metal manufacturing	605	1.3097	0.1679	3.6019	792	102	2
11. Fabricated metal product manufacturing	11,785	1.5478	0.3562	9.3663	18,241	4,198	110
12. Machinery manufacturing	11,943	1.5211	0.3384	9.4022	18,167	4,042	112
13. Computer and electronic product manufacturing	58,748	1.8516	0.6306	17.3905	108,778	37,047	1,022
14. Electrical equipment and appliance manufacturing	21,710	1.6644	0.4204	11.8733	36,134	9,127	258
15. Motor vehicle, body, trailer, and parts manufacturing	110,908	1.5815	0.3529	8.8123	175,401	39,139	977
16. Other transportation equipment manufacturing	95,197	1.7794	0.6220	13.5249	169,393	59,212	1,288
17. Furniture and related product manufacturing	34,592	1.7311	0.4324	12.628	59,882	14,957	437
18. Miscellaneous manufacturing	53,071	1.7829	0.5320	15.9414	94,620	28,234	846
19. Food, beverage, and tobacco product manufacturing	254,246	1.8828	0.3845	11.666	478,695	97,758	2,966
20. Textile and textile product mills	17,049	1.6715	0.4289	12.0428	28,498	7,312	205
21. Apparel, leather, and allied product manufacturing	69,824	1.8387	0.5998	27.0256	128,386	41,881	1,887
22. Paper manufacturing	10,226	1.6071	0.3567	8.6776	16,434	3,648	89
23. Printing and related support activities	1,727	1.7738	0.5417	16.4828	3,064	936	28
24. Petroleum and coal products manufacturing	271,542	1.3507	0.2088	3.3821	366,771	56,698	918
25. Chemical manufacturing	119,735	1.6249	0.3168	6.75	194,557	37,932	808
26. Plastics and rubber products manufacturing	13,576	1.5286	0.3211	9.1577	20,752	4,359	124
27. Wholesale trade	235,366	1.8397	0.5702	14.5997	433,004	134,206	3,436
28. Retail trade	532,249	1.9281	0.5916	22.3148	1,026,229	314,878	11,877
29. Air transportation	45,595	2.036	0.4955	13.3201	92,832	22,593	607
30. Rail transportation	3,778	1	0.0000	0	3,778	0	—
31. Water transportation	15,698	2.1097	0.4502	12.3416	33,118	7,067	194

Table D.3—Continued

	Revised Allocation (thousands of $2006)	Final-Demand Output ($)	Final-Demand Earnings ($)	Final-Demand Employment (jobs/$million)	Final-Demand Output ($thousands)	Final-Demand Earnings ($thousands)	Final-Demand Employment (jobs)
32. Truck transportation	28,446	2.0269	0.5976	15.805	57,657	16,999	450
33. Transit and ground passenger transportation	12,229	2.1047	0.6995	40.9574	25,738	8,554	501
34. Pipeline transportation	369	1.7057	0.3055	6.2986	629	113	2
35. Other transportation and support activities	32,064	2.0235	0.7953	19.4377	64,882	25,501	623
36. Warehousing and storage	6,292	1.9659	0.7477	24.1407	12,370	4,705	152
37. Publishing including software	34,764	1.7848	0.4949	12.4276	62,047	17,205	432
38. Motion picture and sound recording industries	14,722	1.9458	0.4477	18.6018	28,647	6,591	274
39. Broadcasting and telecommunications	107,667	1.9822	0.3835	8.9783	213,418	41,290	967
40. Information and data processing services	11,958	1.9949	0.4971	14.0097	23,855	5,944	168
41. Federal Reserve banks, credit intermed., and related services	125,579	1.6245	0.4483	11.241	204,003	56,297	1,412
42. Securities, commodity contracts, investments	52,273	2.0582	0.7422	24.2209	107,587	38,797	1,266
43. Insurance carriers and related activities	154,802	2.0526	0.5624	13.6606	317,748	87,061	2,115
44. Funds, trusts, and other financial vehicles	50,878	1.7423	0.4374	9.6151	88,645	22,254	489
45. Real estate	506,139	1.555	0.2317	8.6217	787,046	117,272	4,364
46. Rental and leasing services and lessors of intangible assets	37,983	2.1888	0.5105	16.4569	83,137	19,390	625
47. Professional, scientific, and technical services	507,350	2.0785	0.7421	19.061	1,054,528	376,505	9,671
48. Management of companies and enterprises	0	2.097	0.7024	14.7166	0	0	—
49. Administrative and support services	200,691	2.0679	0.7226	27.6549	415,008	145,019	5,550
50. Waste management and remediation services	69,988	2.0577	0.5468	14.1446	144,015	38,270	990
51. Educational services	129,779	2.1536	0.7640	29.5122	279,493	99,151	3,830
52. Ambulatory healthcare services	183,191	2.0504	0.7583	18.7241	375,616	138,914	3,430
53. Hospitals and nursing and residential care facilities	137,539	2.1323	0.7522	20.3823	293,275	103,457	2,803
54. Social assistance	63,742	2.079	0.7400	33.668	132,520	47,169	2,146
55. Performing arts, museums, and related activities	20,021	2.0669	0.7335	44.5509	41,381	14,685	892
56. Amusements, gambling, and recreation	75,069	1.881	0.5617	22.1301	141,205	42,166	1,661
57. Accommodation	60,783	1.8973	0.5547	18.3948	115,323	33,716	1,118
58. Food services and drinking places	265,720	1.9379	0.5321	26.0724	514,938	141,389	6,928
59. Other services	285,793	2.0408	0.5778	20.3042	583,246	165,131	5,803
60. Households	7,935	1.3174	0.3707	12.1654	10,453	2,941	97
Total	6,147,812				11,510,347	3,302,743	101,532

References

BEA—see U.S. Department of Commerce, Bureau of Economic Analysis.

Bonds, Timothy M., Myron Hura, and Thomas-Durell Young, *Enhancing Army Joint Force Headquarters Capabilities*, Santa Monica, Calif.: RAND Corporation, MG-675-A, 2010. As of April 20, 2011:
http://www.rand.org/pubs/monographs/MG675.html

Defense Manpower Data Center (DMDC), *Atlas*, 2009. As of April 20, 2011:
http://siadapp.dmdc.osd.mil/personnel/L03/fy09/atlas_2009.pdf

Defense Travel Management Office (DTMO), "BAH Calculator," web page, undated. As of April 20, 2011:
http://www.defensetravel.dod.mil/site/bahCalc.cfm

———, "Overseas COLA Calculator," web page, undated. As of February 2011:
http://www.defensetravel.dod.mil/site/colaCalc.cfm

———, "Per Diem Rates Query," web page, undated. As of February 2011:
http://www.defensetravel.dod.mil/site/perdiemCalc.cfm

Federal Procurement Data System – Next Generation, online database, undated. As of April 20, 2011:
https://www.fpds.gov/fpdsng_cms/

Harrell, Margaret C., Nelson Lim, Laura Werber Castaneda, and Daniela Golinelli, *Working Around the Military: Challenges to Military Spouse Employment and Education*, Santa Monica, Calif.: RAND Corporation, MG-196-OSD, 2004. As of April 20, 2011:
http://www.rand.org/pubs/monographs/MG196.html

Hickam Air Force Base, *Economic Impact Statement*, 2008.

Hosek, James, Beth J. Asch, C. Christine Fair, Craig Martin, and Michael Mattock, *Married to the Military: The Employment and Earnings of Military Wives Compared with Those of Civilian Wives*, Santa Monica, Calif.: RAND Corporation, MR-1565-OSD, 2002. As of April 8, 2011:
http://www.rand.org/pubs/monograph_reports/MR1565.html

Hosek, James, and Francisco Martorell, *How Have Deployments During the War on Terrorism Affected Reenlistment?* Santa Monica, Calif.: RAND Corporation, MG-873-OSD, 2009. As of April 20, 2011:
http://www.rand.org/pubs/monographs/MG873.html

Office of the Deputy Assistant Secretary of Defense for Military Community and Family Policy (MC&FP), "Military Installations," Hickam Air Force Base website profile, 2011. As of April 20, 2011:
http://www.militaryinstallations.dod.mil/pls/psgprod/f?p=MI:CONTENT:0::::P4_INST_ID,P4_
CONTENT_TITLE,P4_CONTENT_EKMT_ID,P4_CONTENT_DIRECTORY:2140,Government%20
Housing,30.90.60.30.90.0.0.0.0,8

Office of the Deputy Under Secretary of Defense, Installations and Environment (OUSD I&E), Military Housing Privatization, "Housing Projects Hawaii," web page, undated. As of April 20, 2011:
http://www.acq.osd.mil/housing/state_hi.htm

Ruggles, Steven, J. Trent Alexander, Katie Genadek, Ronald Goeken, Matthew B. Schroeder, and Matthew Sobek, *Integrated Public Use Microdata Series: Version 5.0* [Machine-readable database], Minneapolis, Minn.: University of Minnesota, 2010. As of April 20, 2011:
http://usa.ipums.org/usa/

Sasaki, Kyohei, "Military Expenditures and the Employment Multiplier in Hawaii," *The Review of Economics and Statistics*, Vol. 45, No. 3, 1963, pp. 298–304.

State of Hawaii, Department of Business, Economic Development, and Tourism, *Quarterly Statistical and Economic Report (QSER), 1st Quarter, 2011*, 2011. As of April 20, 2011:
http://hawaii.gov/dbedt/info/economic/data_reports/qser/archive-qser/qser-2011q1.pdf

———, "State of Hawaii Data Book," website, various years. As of April 20, 2011:
http://hawaii.gov/dbedt/info/economic/databook/

U.S. Census Bureau, "American Community Survey," website, undated. As of April 20, 2011:
http://www.census.gov/acs/www/

U.S. Department of Commerce, Bureau of Economic Analysis, *Regional Multipliers: A User Handbook for the Regional Input-Output Modeling System (RIMS II)*, 1997. As of April 20, 2011:
http://www.bea.gov/scb/pdf/regional/perinc/meth/rims2.pdf

———, "Regional Multipliers from the Regional Input-Output Modeling System (RIMS II): A Brief Description," web page, undated. As of April 20, 2011:
http://www.bea.gov/regional/rims/brfdesc.cfm

U.S. Department of Defense (DoD), Office of the Actuary, *Military Retirement Fund Valuation Report, FY 2000*. As of April 20, 2011:
http://actuary.defense.gov/wholebook.pdf

U.S. Department of Education, *Impact Aid, Fiscal Year 2010 Budget Request*, 2009. As of April 20, 2011:
http://www2.ed.gov/about/overview/budget/budget10/justifications/b-impactaid.pdf

U.S. Department of Labor, Bureau of Labor Statistics, "Consumer Expenditure Survey," website, undated. As of April 20, 2011:
http://www.bls.gov/cex/

U.S. Office of Personnel Management, "2009 Plan Information for Hawaii," web page, undated. As of April 20, 2011:
http://www.opm.gov/insure/health/planinfo/2009/states/hi.asp